FUNNY MONEY

Other Books by the Same Author

Agenda: A Plan for Action (1971)

Exit Inflation (1981)

Jobs For All: Capitalism on Trail (1984)

Canada at the Crossroads (1990)
(Le Canada à Son Carrefour)

Damn the Torpedoes (1990)

FUNNY MONEY

A COMMON SENSE ALTERNATIVE
TO MAINLINE ECONOMICS

PAUL HELLYER

Chimo Media

Canadian Cataloguing in Publication Data

Hellyer, Paul, 1923 -
  Funny money

Includes bibliographical reference and index.
ISBN 0-9694394-2-3

1. Macroeconomics I. Title.

HB172.5.H45 1994   339   C94-932482-5

Printed and bound in Canada. The paper used in this book is acid free.

Chimo Media Limited
99 Atlantic Avenue, Suite 302
Toronto, ON ˙ M6K 3J8
Canada

CONTENTS

FOR

THE FAMILY OF MAN

ACKNOWLEDGMENTS

A number of individuals and organizations have assisted in the preparation of this book and I am deeply grateful to them.

I am indebted to Susan Bellan, Bill Bussiere, Jordan Grant, Wm. Hixson, Bill Krehm and professors John Hotson and W.H. Pope for reading the manuscript. They made innumerable suggestions of immense value as to how the material might be presented. While they also helped me to avoid many errors and omissions, responsibility for those that slipped through the net, and for the positions taken, is mine alone.

My able research assistant, Jan Mathys Willems, proved to be an invaluable resource. He was able to trace and find the most illusive information. He also prepared the tables and figures which help illustrate some of the most important points in my thesis.

Nina Moskaliuk, my executive assistant, deserves a special word of praise. She was painstaking in her research and verification of facts and references as well as indefatigable in recording and revising the text chapter by chapter.

Andy Donato wins the prize for his brilliantly expressive and insightful cartoon. In one picture he has captured the essence of a thousand words because it is, after all, the naked truth that we are looking for.

Of the organizations which assisted, the parliamentary library in Ottawa, the John Robarts and Metro Reference libraries in Toronto, the United States Consulate in Toronto and the United Kingdom High Commission in Ottawa were especially cooperative and helpful. To each and all my grateful thanks.

Finally, my eternal gratitude to my family and especially to my dear wife Ellen for tolerating my lifelong obsession as I go charging off to the ramparts one more time. I hope the day will come when you will feel that it has all been worthwhile.

INTRODUCTION

"A person who has ceased learning ought not to be allowed to wander around loose in these dangerous times. "

Anononymous

Your reaction to this book will probably be the best test you will ever have as to whether or not your mind is open to new ideas which challenge a lifetime of intellectual and social conditioning.

Do you know why we had a Great Depression in the 1930's? Did it need to happen? Why have there been a number of recessions since the end of World War II including the last two devastating ones in 1981-82 and 1990-91. Were they really necessary?

Have you ever asked yourself why it is that in a depression or a recession when there are unemployed carpenters, plumbers, electricians, cabinet-makers, farmers, health-care workers, teachers and environmental scientists on the one hand, just to mention a few, that on the other hand there are people in desperate need of housing, clothing, food, literacy training and medical attention? Why are we making such slow progress in cleaning up the air we breathe and the water we drink?

Even more perplexing, have you ever wondered why almost all governments are deeply in debt and getting in deeper all the time? Why is it that they have to cut back essential programs when the need is so great? Do you also wonder why young people, in particular, express a sense of hopelessness and doubt that their future will be as bright as that enjoyed by their parents?

The fundamental reason for all of this irrationality is that our monetary and banking system, stripped of all the snake oil and holy water that has been poured on it over the years, is nothing more than the perpetuation of a scam invented by the English goldsmiths more than three hundred years ago. It is an unjust and unsustainable system which has to be reformed if capitalism is to survive and prosper.

Bluntly stated, there has never been a depression or a recession that was necessary. They have all been, basically, monetary phenomena flowing from a profound lack of understanding of monetary theory on the part of the economics profession. Two hundred years after James Watt's adaptation of the steam engine and the industrial revolution changed, for all time, the order of magnitude of the potential for producing goods, economists still haven't designed a complementary system of distribution. Mainline economists haven't managed to negotiate and safely exit from the labyrinth of change. They are still lost in the maze of mirrors.

Don't get me wrong. Many great economists have played on the world stage and deserve their recognized place in history. I have read dozens of their most important works and have often been in total awe of the formidable intellects of the authors. Their mastery of microeconomics is unquestioned and of immense value in attempting to understand the subject.

When it comes to macroeconomics, however, there is less consensus. I am equally awestruck by the complicated mathematical formulae and the ingenious abstractions of specialists in this field. When I put their books down, however, I think how detached many of them are from the real world of political economy. Generation after generation goes by and we still don't have a theory, or combination of theories, which will allow us to achieve and maintain full employment in the absence of significant inflation. Indeed many economists, influenced more by economic history than mathematical certainty, deny that such a state is possible – except, perhaps, in the short run.

To confirm this opinion I read the *Fortune Encyclopedia of Economics* to refresh my memory. The brief summaries of the major schools of thought, though interesting, left me with that same empty feeling that I have felt for so long.   The neoclassical, new classical macroeconomics and monetarist schools can all be dismissed as inadequate because they are based on a hypothetical "price-auction" economy which, to the extent it may have existed at one time, has long since ceased to exist.   They offer no hope and no solutions for the real economy.

Keynesian and neo Keynesian models are closer to reality when they accept the downward stickiness of wages and prices; but they, too, have failed to recognize the preponderant influence of monopoly power as the source of contemporary inflation.   This results in a tolerance of involuntary unemployment which is unnaturally and unnecessarily high. In addition, Keynesians, like their classical, neo classical and monetarist homologues, have failed to address the monetary and banking issues which are leading to an unsustainable burden of debt.   In effect, then, there is no major economic school offering workable solutions to the real problems of the real economy.   Little wonder that young people, sensing that this is true, have been losing hope.

A root problem is that economics is very much like theology.   If the prevailing theory says that the sun revolves around the earth, the sun revolves around the earth.   Rational discussion is neither encouraged nor welcome.   It's the economic "seminarians" against the world.

About twenty years ago I sent an outline of a book on economic reform to Doubleday in New York in the hope they would agree to publish it.   Several weeks later I received a letter of rejection which stated: "Our editors believe that the economists can't all be wrong."   Throughout the years I have consoled myself with the thought that had Galileo sent Doubleday an outline of his thesis that the earth revolves around the sun he would have received a letter back saying: "Our editors believe that the bishops can't all be wrong."   History will show that, notwithstanding the judgment of Doubleday editors, the mainline economists were wrong and that millions of people have suffered, needlessly, as a result.

In contrast to mainline economics there have always been a few mavericks on the macroeconomic side who deserve a special place in heaven for their pioneering efforts; and there are some living today who have been fighting a courageous lop-sided battle in an attempt to persuade the world to listen. They deserve a special award for valor because they have been perceived as the lunatic fringe of economics when in fact they have been the sane fringe of a lunatic profession. Some of them have been a great source of support and encouragement to me in writing this book.

For more than two decades I have been proposing a simple but potentially effective incomes policy as a gentler, fairer way of controlling the wage-price spiral than the horrendous recessions we have been forced to endure. In a sentence, it is the imposition of guidelines to limit the abuse of monopoly power on the part of big business and big labor. Had the suggestion been implemented prior to the last two major recessions, as an alternative to the monetarist approach which has been comparable to using a bulldozer instead of a hoe to weed a flower garden, it would have been possible to achieve acceptable levels of employment and balanced budgets without significant inflation. The situation today would have been as summer compared to winter – though still less than ideal.

Now, however, with the near-universal increase in deficits and debt, more heroic measures are required. For the first time since the Great Depression of the 1930's non-revolutionary measures appear to be inadequate. We have to change our monetary system. If we do that, in conjunction with the incomes policy I have espoused, the capitalist system will work admirably. The two reforms are as complementary as love and marriage or apple pie and cheese.

What I will propose is a proper marriage between the financial economy and the real economy of goods and services. The importance of the marriage was underlined in a March 14, 1994 *New York Times* article entitled "Big Economies Turn to the Jobs Issue", in advance of the first Group of Seven financial conference ever to include labor ministers. It read, in part: "We used to think that jobs and the economy were the same thing", the United States Secretary of Labor, Robert B. Reich, said: "But we have learned in recent years that the paper economy and the people's economy are not always the same thing."

Indeed they are not! But the most significant aspect of Mr. Reich's statement is recognition of that fundamental fact. To the best of my knowledge it was the first time anyone of cabinet rank publicly acknowledged that there are two economies and that one may be out of sync with the other.

That is the bed-rock on which I will build. Friends familiar with my work will know that for the chapters on economic analysis and the incomes policy I have borrowed extensively from previous books on the same subject. When it comes to the principal thrust of monetary reform, however, what I have to say is all new for me. Although I have recognized the need since university days, I have not, until now, been brave enough to put my thoughts on paper.

This book, therefore, will be my "coming out of the closet, economically", so to speak. It will not only attempt to answer the questions posed earlier, it will be even more specific. I will argue that a happy, common sense marriage of the real and paper economies, including monetary reform and a non-inflationary incomes policy, will allow the governments of industrialized countries to:

1. stimulate their economies to the point where they are operating at or near their potential;

2. achieve and maintain full employment;

3. achieve and maintain price stability simultaneously with the achievement of full employment, where the number of job seekers and the number of job openings is roughly in equilibrium;

4. balance their budgets;

5. reduce their indebtedness;

6. maintain the range of common services they provide; and, finally,

7. one fine day, perhaps, reduce taxes.

The term "business cycle" should disappear from the economic lexicon.

With such an inclusive list one could be forgiven, at this stage, for believing that some sort of magic is required. Not so! All that is required is a <u>large dose</u> of common sense. Consequently, the text that follows is written for ordinary people with common sense. It contains only two simple equations so you don't need a PhD in economics to understand it. A good grasp of arithmetic, however, will be helpful.

At first blush it may strike you as odd that a Canadian should be writing for a primarily American audience. I make no apology, however, because the subject matter is universal and the influence of the U.S. economy on other economies, especially that of its neighbor, Canada, is quite overwhelming. Much of my anxiety, then, stems from the fact that the policies currently being followed in the U.S. fill me with foreboding. The Fed's fifth interest rate increase in the first eight months of 1994 was the final straw. Hailed as "aggressive and decisive" it merely underlined the disastrous gulf between the paper economy of the financiers and people's real needs. The long-term cost to the U.S. and world economies will be enormous - so great, in fact, that the subversive aspects of a policy which attempts to control inflation by means of interest rates alone must be addressed at once, before it is too late.

Finally, I must admit at the outset that I have not included the inevitable exceptions that test every general rule. To do so would be tedious for me and deter far too many potential readers from persisting to the end. I must be forgiven, too, for failing to bow the knee to political correctness. My knees are not as supple as they once were and what I have to say is designed to benefit everyone without distinction of group, race, gender or class. It should provide a ray of hope for all.

CHAPTER 1

A TRAGIC DIVORCE

"Everything's got a moral, if you can only find it."

Lewis Carroll

Would you believe that a divorce which happened more than 200 years ago would have earth-shaking consequences from that era right down to the present. Well, that's the way I see it.

The industrial revolution which began in England in the latter half of the eighteenth century changed, for all time, the order of magnitude of the potential for the production of new goods. Letting machines do much of the work that had previously been done by men and women increased output in a way that was unprecedented since the beginning of recorded time. The extensive use of real capital increased the efficiency of labor and those countries which exploited this advantage would never be the same again.

To maximize the potential, however, someone had to design a new system of distribution that would complement the increase in industrial capacity. The old system of barter, which had been supplemented from time immemorial by the use of

1

gold, silver, and copper coins, proved totally inadequate to cope with the new volume of transactions. So it became necessary to invent new forms of "money" to make the system work. More than two centuries of ad hocary in this area contain all of the elements of comedy and tragedy as well as thievery. Sometimes the real economies operated at their full potential – usually when there had been a fresh infusion of money of one kind or another. This was especially true in time of war. On the other hand there were long periods of stagnation and high unemployment when an economy was starved for cash. This roller-coaster of robust growth followed by recession or depression became endemic to the system. Unlike the fat and lean years of Biblical record, when Joseph used his insider's knowledge of an impending natural phenomenon to great advantage, there is nothing natural about business cycles. Even a cursory reading of economic history shows that they have been the children of the divorce between the real and financial economies which resulted in alternate periods of too much and then too little money in the system. It is a history of overindulgence followed by excessive dieting leading to anorexia. Instead of a sane and balanced diet, two centuries of monetary history reveal the split personality which caused the estrangement of the two economies.

Using the marriage analogy, there have been many flirtations, a few torrid affairs, in wartime and when Europe imported gold and silver from the new world and, one might say, a 15 year period of trial cohabitation from roughly 1950-1965 when Keynes ruled supreme. But even this unofficial honeymoon didn't last and was followed by another parting of the ways. Seldom has any relationship been so rocky.

While the consequences of the boom-bust cycle are usually spoken or written about in economic or social terms, less has been said about the political consequences. These cycles reinforced the split between left and right in politics and contributed greatly to the division between East and West in the cold war.

In the view of the well-known economist Joseph Schumpeter, and others, Karl Marx was not a reformer whose greatest contribution was in the field of economics. He either did not understand or refused to recognize the very large contribution of capital goods in the production process. Reading Marx's *Das Kapital* one cannot escape the conclusion that he was primarily a theologian, in the sense that he spent tremendous energy constructing abstractions which gain absolute credibility by the simple device of ignoring economic realities. In this sense he was not unlike the classical economists who had influenced him so greatly.

Although it was capital and its owners, "the capitalists", who became the focus of Marx's fury, it was the degradation of the working classes and the periodic economic crises that influenced him profoundly and provided the driving motive for his work. Like Rodbertus before him, and hundreds of other economists since, Marx thought that "the capitalist continually tended to produce more than the market for his goods would absorb. Products would not automatically be 'cleared' as in a natural or barter economy."[1] In *Ideas of the Great Economists*, George Soule goes on to say: "This was the cause of the frequently recurring periods in which a surplus of goods in the hands of the capitalist was accompanied by unemployment and want on the part of the workers. Though Marx's theory of depression was a crude and incomplete one, he deserves credit as one of the first economic theorists to emphasize an obviously critical defect in the operation of a capitalist order."[2]

It is a tragedy that having recognized an inherent defect in the capitalist system Marx failed to apply his intellect and energy toward the elimination of that defect. Instead he sought to replace it with a totally different system with defects too fundamental to be exorcized by moderate reform.

SOCIALISM'S FAILURE

Socialism is pure and beautiful in theory and totally impractical in practice on any major scale. It was practiced by adherents to the early Christian church who "had all things common, and sold their possessions and goods, and divided them among all, as anyone had need."[3] There is no evidence as to how well the system worked but we do know that the practice exists today in sects like the Hutterites and some Mennonites. They limit the size of their colonies, however, because they have learned from experience that discipline can only be applied effectively to limited numbers.

Israel, too, has applied the principle in a number of its Kibbutzim. There is no doubt that the idealistic image has been and remains a powerful force in draining the swamps and making the desert bloom like a rose. There is also little doubt that the pioneering communal farm movement is suffering a major identity crisis. In a full page report by Bob Hepburn of the *Toronto Star's* Mideast Bureau we read: "Many are in deep financial trouble and some of the traditional institutions of kibbutz life are evolving or being abandoned entirely. Economic reality and individual demands are replacing socialistic values and the ideal of a sharing, co-operative society. In short, life on the kibbutz isn't what it used to be."[4]

The application of socialism runs into problems on two fundamental fronts. It implies the perfectibility of man and there is precious little empirical evidence in support of that dream. I have known a handful of people who come about as close as the theory demands. But they are a tiny minority – perhaps one or two percent. Most of us, including many who might be considered both compassionate and generous, reach the stage where we'll rebel at working another hour or paying more tax to pamper some lazy lout who insists on spending his days fishing.

The other drawback to the large scale application of socialism, or state-capitalism which is a more accurate label for the Eastern-European experiments, is centralized decision making. Its stale-dated snail's pace is no competition for the genius of privately-administered capitalism with its fast-moving, decentralized decision-making process.

In the former U.S.S.R., I was told, the allocation of peanut butter, jam and marmalade for every restaurant was made in Moscow. If the good burghers of Minsk preferred more marmalade and less peanut butter than the national average, too bad. They would have a chronic shortage of one while the surplus peanut butter turned rancid. A privately-run eatery normally adjusts to the tastes of its clients.

I can give dozens of examples of private and public decision-making from personal experience but one on each side of the argument will suffice for purposes of illustration. My wife and I own a small tourist resort in the lake country north of Toronto.[5] On an inspection tour one spring some years ago we noted that the furniture in the lounge needed replacing and that we needed additional docking space for boats. Within 48 hours the new furniture was in place and the following day a local carpenter had begun to build the dock.

The disadvantage of centralized decision-making was underlined for me when I became Minister of Transport with responsibility for the National Harbours Board. The Board operated ports on both coasts which had been locally administered before the depression of the 1930's but which came under federal administration when the port authorities defaulted on their debt. During a discussion about returning some facilities to local authorities I was given a powerful case history in support of decentralization. The story involved a request from the Port of Vancouver to buy a second container crane at a time when containers were rapidly gaining in popularity. By the time the Harbours Board approved the purchase, 18 months after the request was made, most of the extra business had gone to Seattle. This was good luck for our U.S. neighbors but it was a perfect example of how a rigid system can hamstring the ability to compete.

It was the inherent rigidity of the Soviet brand of socialism, or state capitalism, which led to its downfall after 70 years of experimentation. Too many bureaucrats making too many decisions about too many subjects about which they knew too little – and taking too long to do it. Eventually the frustration at the working level was palpable.

I remember having breakfast at a Kiev hotel one morning some years ago when a local gentleman came to my table and asked if he could join me. As I was on a tour of discovery I was more than delighted to agree. Later he asked if he could pay for my breakfast and I declined with thanks but wondered why it shouldn't be the other way around. He said that he was in charge of a dairy herd at a nearby collective farm and consequently was well paid. He had lots of rubles in the bank but there was nothing in the stores to buy. It would be easy for him to increase productivity by 20 percent, he said, and earn a substantial bonus; but what was the point when he already had more cash than he could reasonably spend.

I am sure my friend would have been glad to see the system collapse. Certainly there was great rejoicing in the West which couldn't dare to hope for a near-bloodless counter-revolution on such a massive scale. Expectations soared on both sides of the old iron curtain. But, as recent elections in Russia and Hungary have shown, some of the cheering may be premature. The victory may be tentative. Dependency is not easily broken, especially when the door of opportunity has not yet opened except for a small, venturesome and fortunate minority. Mass unemployment, and the freedom to be hungry, isn't a happy alternative to memories of jobs and food – albeit at near subsistence levels. The choice can lead to volatility.

This concern was raised by Irish President Mary Robinson during a two-day visit to Toronto in August 1994. She said that democratic countries must offer real help to Eastern European countries or risk "the pendulum of history swinging back to darker days." A civil liberties lawyer and long-time member of the Irish Senate prior to her election as president in 1990, Ms. Robinson cautioned there may only be "a limited opportunity" to proffer such support. "Failure risks the pendulum of history swinging violently back to darker days, so starkly illustrated for us by the tragedy in the former Yugoslavia ... we cannot remain indifferent or detached."[6]

The inability of the Western world to provide substantial aid through the transition phase has made a bad situation worse. Economic mismanagement on a massive scale has made the West impotent to act aggressively and decisively. The let-down is grist for the mill of the Marxist rear-guard. Why, they ask, would you want to emulate a system as unpredictable and problem-ridden as Western capitalism which can't get its own act together. Even its boosters have to admit that the record of the privately-administered capitalist system has been far less than perfect.

Marx assumed that capitalism was inherently exploitive and would never work to the benefit of the common man, and while it is easy to come to that conclusion from studying the earliest years of the industrial age, the evidence suggests that it wasn't long before incomes began to rise dramatically. This continued, though far from consistently, until post World War II industrial workers enjoyed a standard of living that would have been the envy of many ancient kings and princes. That is the upside. The downside is that not everyone has been so lucky and, as a result of the last two recessions, restructuring, downsizing, rationalization and globalization, a growing sense of insecurity has crept into the public psyche. People, especially young people, are apprehensive and wonder aloud what the future holds.

CAPITALISM'S WEAKNESS

The social unrest caused by high unemployment has not been limited to countries of the former Soviet bloc. The 1981-82 recession caused race riots amongst disenchanted youth in London, England. The most recent debacle of 1990-91, and since, has led to a resurgence of neo-nazism in Germany, and the emergence of ugly, white-supremacist youth groups in both Canada and the U.S. When things go wrong people look for scapegoats, usually immigrants or those of a different race, religion or color. In such circumstances one begins to wonder when, if ever, we will have a system which is stable and which renews hope for the young of diverse origins.

The events which give rise to the continuing debate about the superiority of systems would probably never have arisen had the divorce between the real and the financial economies not occurred. Periodic depressions and recessions have always been unnerving and poured fuel on the fires of controversy between thinkers on the "left" and "right". Both sides claimed they wanted the same things - jobs for people who wanted to work, adequate food and respectable housing for all, fairness and stability.   Each thought they had the answers though neither was able to deliver the promises implicit in their rhetoric.   With socialism the miracle was just around the corner.   With privately-administered capitalism every new high raised hopes of continuous improvement only to have those hopes shattered when the seemingly inevitable downturn occurred.

Often there were ordinary citizens who insisted that the problem was a periodic shortage of purchasing power in the system and that something should be done about it.   This was usually denied by economists who fell back on Say's law, i.e. that all production creates an equal and opposite demand and therefore there could be no such thing as a periodic shortage of purchasing power.   It was not until John Maynard Keynes, a respected member of the economics club, said that of course there was a periodic shortage of purchasing power that the economics profession began to recognize the obvious.   This was about the time of my introduction to economic reality.

I was raised during the Great Depression of the 1930's, which I remember well.   The images of destitute men coming to our farm house door and being fed by my mother are still vivid in my memory.   So is the sight of one of my cousins, an insurance salesman, putting new cardboard liners in his shoes to cover the holes in the soles and protect his feet from the elements.   It was a time of desperation and so well recorded and remembered that there is no need for me to elaborate here; but it was this first-hand experience in the 1930's that was the basis for the formation of the 64 trillion dollar question.   Why? Why have there been extended periods when human and material resources have been wasted, shamelessly?

That was the question I kept asking at university at the end of World War II when I was taking advantage of veterans' benefits to complete my education.   I felt compelled to ask my professors if recessions and depressions were really necessary and inevitable.   Invariably the replies were far from satisfactory.   Each, in his own way, conveyed the clear impression that recessions and depressions were inherent to the system and, for that reason, inevitable. When I asked them why, however, they didn't know.   Usually I got a lecture in economic history which was an unsatisfactory substitute for plausible theory.   To test the depth of the boom-bust orthodoxy I conducted an unofficial poll of 15 senior students in economics and asked them the same question.   The result was identical. Every one of the fifteen, without exception, either quoted or paraphrased the same paragraph from the textbook that they were using.

It didn't take me long to develop a contrary view. Intuition told me that the boom-bust cycle didn't make any sense in a diverse industrial economy and I eventually came to the conclusion that in every case the cycles had been monetary phenomena.   In all likelihood there had never been a recession or depression that was either necessary or inevitable.   The only reason that they became inevitable was the lack of understanding of monetary theory and the essential role that money plays in the operation of an economy.   Money was the problem – the principal cause of each acceleration or deceleration of the economic roller-coaster.

While the love of money may be the root of all evil, it has been mass confusion about what money is and does that has wreaked more havoc than this world knows of.   Untold numbers of farmers losing their farms, sometimes after many generations in the family; untold numbers of businesses going bankrupt, unnecessarily; untold numbers of people losing their houses when they haven't been able to pay the interest rates on their mortgages; and millions upon millions of people unemployed, involuntarily, because there have been no jobs for them to go to.   All of this in addition to the albatross that has been hung around the neck of Third World countries by the usurious interest rates charged on monies advanced to them by the industrialized world.   The totality of the evil consequences caused by the divorce between the real economies and financial economies of the world is beyond either comprehension or calculation.   So the least we should do is begin to try to understand what money is and where it comes from.   That, in itself, is no mean task.

CHAPTER 2

MONEY, FUNNY MONEY AND PHONY MONEY

"A national debt, if it is not excessive, will be to us a national blessing."

Alexander Hamilton

Where do babies come from? I can still remember some childhood discussions on the subject and some of the vague and inconclusive answers that were bandied about. Babies were found in cabbage patches. On other occasions it was a stork that brought them, though the connection between storks and cabbage patches was never too precise. By the time we reached puberty most of us knew that mummys' tummies had something to do with the wondrous process.

Those nebulous views belonged to the pre-television age. Today ten year olds can get a pretty good sense of it all by watching Murphy Brown on TV. Other programs have actually shown live births which leave nothing to the imagination. You might expect, then, that most people would be equally well informed about where money comes from. Alas that is not the case.

In the course of writing this book I asked scores of friends and associates – not including my circle of economist friends who are well versed in the subject – if they knew where money comes from. The sample included people with BAs, MAs, PhDs, DDs, BScs, MScs, and lots of ordinary 'folk' with vast experience and much common sense. Not one of them had what I would call a working knowledge of the subject. Even more surprising, this was true of some who write columns and editorials on the subjects of money and economics in order to inform (or misinform) their readers about preferred priorities in public policy. This chapter and the next will attempt to expose readers to at least a rudimentary knowledge of what money is and where it comes from. It is time that we removed the veil separating us from the financial holy of holies and see what the high priests of monetary orthodoxy do back there.

What is money? It is a good question for which there is no easy answer! It has meant different things to different people in different cultures in different times. Its importance was recognized in the Bible which refers to money more than seventy times. In those days money usually meant copper, silver or gold coins. An exception, and one of the earliest recorded examples of a breakdown in the monetary system, occurred during the seven year famine recorded in Genesis. As Pharaoh's administrator, Joseph had accumulated all the money in both Egypt and Canaan in exchange for grain. But the people were still hungry so they came to Joseph and said, "Give us bread, for why should we die in your presence? For the money has failed." Joseph agreed to give them bread in exchange for livestock which became a substitute for money – an early example of mobile, liquid capital.[1]

A dual system of metallic coins and barter acted as the principal financial instruments worldwide for centuries. The first deviation from this appears to have occurred in China where they invented fei-ch'ien (flying money) which they used in a way similar to our bank drafts to send money from one place to another during the T'ang dynasty (A.D. 618-907). Later, when iron coins were the main currency in Szechwan province, the heavy weight led people to deposit them in some proto-banks and use the receipts for financial transactions. Many historians believe that the use of these receipts as a money substitute was the origin of paper money.[2]

For the next two centuries, through changing empires and dynasties, metal money coexisted with paper which had not yet become a national currency.   In 1161, a new kind of money, the hui-tzu, or "check medium" was issued.   It was tightly tied to reserves of copper coins so the exchange rate was kept constant for more than 20 years and it became a truly national currency around the end of the twelfth century.   Then, in a situation that has been repeated innumerable times since, the government resorted to an inflationary policy of printing money to finance two wars.   The inflation beginning in the second half of the twelfth century has been recorded as the first nationwide inflation of paper money in world history.[3]

THE GOLDSMITHS' SCAM

Although European banking can be traced back to Roman times my launching point is the introduction of paper money to England which appears to have begun with the London goldsmiths in the latter half of the 17th century.   Until 1640 it was the custom for wealthy merchants to deposit their excess cash – gold and silver – in the Mint of the Tower of London for safe-keeping.   In that year Charles I seized the privately owned money and destroyed the Mint's reputation as a safe place.   This action forced merchants and traders to seek alternatives and, subsequently, to store their excess money with the goldsmiths of Lombard Street who had already built strong fire-proof boxes for the storage of their own valuables.[4]

The goldsmiths accepted gold deposits for which they issued receipts which were redeemable on demand.   These receipts were passed from hand to hand and were known as goldsmiths notes, the predecessors of banknotes.   The goldsmiths paid interest of 5 percent on their customers' deposits and then lent the money to their more needy customers at exorbitant rates becoming, in fact, pawnbrokers who advanced money against the collateral of valuable property.[5] They also learned that it was possible to make loans in excess of the gold actually held in their vaults because only a small fraction of their depositors attempted to convert their receipts into gold. Thus began the fractional reserve system, the practice of lending "money" that doesn't really exist. It was to become the most profitable scam in the history of mankind. It was also the quick-sand on which the Bank of England was subsequently founded in 1694 – three hundred years ago.

THE BANK OF ENGLAND'S SCAM

The Bank of England was conceived as a solution to a dilemma. King William's War, 1688-1697, had been extremely costly and this resulted in much of England's gold and silver going to the continent in payment of debt. As a result the money supply was sorely depleted and something had to be done to keep the wheels of commerce turning. Someone got the bright idea that establishing a bank might help to fill the void.

At the time the Bank was chartered the scheme involved an initial subscription by its shareholders of £1,200,000 in gold and silver which would be lent to the government at 8 percent. That seems fair enough, although the interest rate was more than ample for a government-guaranteed investment. It was only the beginning, however, because in addition to a £4,000 management fee, the Bank of England was granted an advantage only available to banks and bankers. It was granted authority to issue "banknotes" in an amount equal to its capital and lend the notes into circulation. This was not the first case of paper money issued by private banks in the modern era but it was the first of great and lasting significance in the English-speaking world.[6]

It was the same system developed by the goldsmiths. By lending the same money twice the Bank could double the interest received on its capital. Nice work if you can get it and you can with a bank charter. It is not too surprising, then, that discussions of this advantage encouraged some members of parliament to become shareholders in the Bank. Money lenders learned early, and have never forgotten, that it pays to have friends in parliament.[7]

The first Bank of England banknotes lent into circulation were, in fact, phantom money which I have labeled "phony money" in order to distinguish it from other money. Public acceptance of the banknotes was based on the assumption that they were "as good as gold". Even when the Bank was subsequently authorized to increase the number of banknotes outstanding in proportion to the gold in its vaults the public seemed blithely unaware that the promise "to redeem in gold" was really a sham. The bankers got away with the deception because they knew, like the goldsmiths before them, that only a small fraction of banknote holders would attempt to redeem those notes at any one time. What had begun as a fraud had been legalized and legitimized, but that wasn't enough to protect the beneficiaries from the consequences of their own greed.

There were times when the Bank of England did not have enough gold in reserve to meet the day-to-day demands for conversion and within two years of operation an early "run" on the bank forced it to suspend payments in specie, i.e. in coins as opposed to paper.[8] This was a situation that was to recur periodically through the next three centuries every time a "crisis" occurred as a result of a pressing need to increase the money supply at a rate in excess of the increase in gold and silver reserves, or when banks got too greedy and put credibility to the test.

"By the year 1725 all the basic essentials of the modern financial mechanism were in being" in England.[9] The Bank had increased its capital, its loans to the government, its issues of banknotes, and its "fractional reserves" for redeeming banknotes on demand, that is, the amount of gold the bank kept as a reserve, this being a small fraction of its outstanding banknotes. Most of the start-up problems of the bank had been disposed of and its status as a going concern firmly established. The Bank of England's unique charter gave it a virtual monopoly on banking in London.

This was not the case in other areas. By 1750 there were 12 banks outside London, and this number increased to 150 by 1776, and 721 by 1810.[10] These were called "country banks" and often they kept their reserves in banknotes of the

Bank of England, rather than in gold or silver coins or ingots. "As late as 1826 it was possible for Lord Liverpool to say that the law permitted any shopkeeper, however limited his means, to establish a bank ... and issue banknotes purporting to be payable on demand" in Bank of England notes that were, in turn, payable by the bank in specie on demand.[11] This was a classic example of paper money backed by other paper money – in essence phony money guaranteed by phony money.

Meanwhile on the other side of the Atlantic Ocean both French and English colonies encountered money supply problems and had to innovate as best possible. The French government neglected to meet the monetary needs of New France, as part of Canada was then known, and it was impossible to balance the budget with its heavy naval and military expenditures. Inflation began in 1685 when Intendant de Meulles, in great need of funds, cut playing-cards in four and signed them to serve as cash, and this card money increased in volume.[12]

GOVERNMENT-CREATED MONEY

The English colonial settlers faced comparable problems. Few were independently wealthy and the colonies suffered a chronic and often acute shortage of gold and silver coins. To make matters worse, Britain routinely banned the export of silver and gold to the colonies because it was desperately required as a base for the expansion of the money supply in the mother country. Deprived of support from "mother" England, necessity became the mother of invention.[13]

In 1690, four years before the Bank of England was chartered, the Massachusetts Bay Colony issued its first colonial notes. This, according to one of my American friends, was a consequence of their part in King William's war. Soldiers had been dispatched to invade Canada on the promise that the French had lots of silver, "Beat 'em and get paid that way", is how he told the story. But Quebec did not fall and the Yanks went back to Boston sore, mean, and unpaid. Something had to be done, so the Massachusetts Bay Note, redeemable in gold "sometime," was born. "This was, if not the very first, one of the first cases of government-created paper money of the modern age."[14]

Early in the 18th century, in May 1723, Pennsylvania loaned into circulation, with real estate as security, notes to the amount of £15,000; and another £30,000 was issued in December. It was enacted that, "counterfeiters were to be punished by having both their 'ears cut off', being whipped on the 'bare back with thirty lashes well laid on,' and fined or sold into servitude."[15] While the punishment for counterfeiters seems somewhat extreme by 20th century standards, the issue of notes accomplished its purpose and sparked a revival of the colony's economy. Ship-building prospered and both exports and imports increased markedly.[16]

The experiment was so successful that the number of notes in circulation was increased from £15,000 in early 1723, to £81,500 in 1754 – a growth rate during the thirty-one years of a moderate 5.6 percent. Even Adam Smith, who was not a fan of government-created money, admitted that Pennsylvania's paper currency "is said never to have sunk below the value of the gold and silver which was current in the colony before the first issue of paper money."[17]

As I mentioned at the outset, the Chinese had used paper money centuries earlier, but for our part of the world, as Curtis P. Nettles points out: "Paper currency issued under government auspices originated in the thirteen colonies; and during the 18th century they were the laboratories in which many currency experiments were performed."[18] There were no banks at that time in any of the 13 colonies so all the paper money was created under the authority of the colonial legislatures. In all there were about 250 separate issues of colonial notes between 1690 and 1775 and the system worked just fine when they avoided over or under issue. It also had distinct advantages over bank or coin money. The legislature could spend, lend or transfer the money into circulation, while banks could only lend (or spend their interest earnings back into circulation) and the coin money was always leaving the colonies to pay for imports.

There is no doubt that the 13 colonies were the Western pioneers in the creation of "funny money", the label many skeptics and cynics apply to government-created money. Why they consider it any funnier than the phony money banks create I will never understand. Perhaps they just suffer from a peculiar sense of humor.

Historians usually play down the role of money creation as a causal factor in bringing about the War for Independence. On the other hand, "[Benjamin] Franklin cited restrictions upon paper money as one of the main reasons for the alienation of the American provinces from the mother country."[19] "To a significant extent, the war was fought over the right of the Colonists to create their own money supply.   When the Continental Congress and the states brought forth large issues of their own legal-tender money in 1775, they committed acts so contrary to British laws governing the colonies and so contemptuous and insulting to British sovereignty as to make war inevitable."[20]

When the war began the United Colonies, or the United States, as they came to be called, were really strapped for gold and silver. Their difficulty was compounded by the blockade imposed by the British Navy. At the same time the war had to be financed by one means or another so the separate states, and the United States, acting through the Continental Congress in an act of defiance against King and parliament, continued the policy that they had previously followed when gold was in short supply – they issued paper money. But now there was a difference. Instead of just printing enough to meet the needs of a moderate growth in trade they had to print an amount which, when added to foreign borrowing and the receipts from taxation, was sufficient to finance the war. Inevitably that amount ceased to have any relation to the increase in output of goods and services and the paper began to lose its value. In 1784 Benjamin Franklin, after defending the necessity of what was done, went on to explain the consequences of excess. "It has been long and often observed, that when the current money of a country is augmented beyond the occasions for money as a medium of commerce, its value as money diminishes...."[21]

It is a truism to which one can say Amen! The amount of money created was so great that its worthlessness was inevitable.

It is noteworthy, however, that much of the hyperinflation of the later years of the Revolution was caused by British counterfeiting in a deliberate attempt to discredit the Continental currency. If that was their aim they succeeded brilliantly but in this particular round of the war over money it was the colonies that had the last laugh. They paid for much of their war effort by issuing "funny" money and the total cost, including interest, until the debt was liquidated, has been estimated as about $250 million. Britain, on the other hand, relied almost entirely on "phony" bank-created borrowed money. "By 1783, the British national debt was roughly $500 million greater than in 1774. But here is the really interesting fact: Britain's national debt has never since 1783 been less than it was at the end of that year."[22] The conclusion that William Hixson draws in his excellent book the *Triumph of the Bankers* (which should be required reading for every student of monetary policy) is that "Britain has not even yet finished paying for the war it lost attempting to suppress the emerging United States."[23] Hixson goes on to say that in the intervening 200 years British taxpayers have paid over $4 billion in interest to their moneylending class of 1783 and its heirs. To add injury to insult, the original $500 million is still outstanding.[24]

While the Americans won that round, future historians may speculate about who "lost" the next one. As a result of the hyperinflation, and the discredited "Continental", Alexander Hamilton, who seemed determined to model the United States monetary and banking system on that of England, was able to get a federal charter for the first Bank of the United States (BUS) and several state banks were chartered. This despite the strongly expressed views of Benjamin Franklin, John Adams and Thomas Jefferson. The Jeffersonians hated the BUS and had it killed after 20 years. Meanwhile the United States didn't create any legal tender paper money from the Revolution until Lincoln's Greenbacks, but this over-reaction exacted a heavy price.

The years immediately following the War for Independence were not happy ones for the people of the United States. The collapse of the monetary system, and the absence of sufficient gold and silver to facilitate trade, caused the country to experience its first great depression. Debtors who had been able to pay creditors with cheap money during the inflationary period now had to pay with money that was scarce and therefore dear. Thus, as Richard B. Morris explains, "each one of the thirteen states found creditors arrayed against debtors."[25] The depression constituted the second half of the lesson in monetary theory. Whereas too much money leads to inflation, too little leads to economic paralysis. Unfortunately these inalienable truths proved to be an insufficient guide for future policy makers.

For almost a hundred years following the War for Independence arguments about "money questions" and the role of banks raged on. Myriad new state banks appeared but when the United States declared war on Britain on June 18, 1812, the task of financing the conflict was considerably more difficult due to the absence of any sort of "central bank". Gold had to be exported to pay for armaments and hoarding was rampant; so except for a few banks in New England most were forced to suspend redemption of their notes on demand, and convertibility was not re-instated until February 1817.[26]

Meanwhile the banking industry was not unaware of the opportunity this presented on the financial side of the economy. The number of banks in the U.S. increased from thirty, in 1800, to seven hundred and thirteen by 1836. By then they had created $306 million in banknotes, plus deposits, but had only about $40 million in gold in their vaults. The ratio for the banks total liabilities – bank notes plus deposits – to metallic reserves was just about seven and a half to one.[27]

Although regulation of the banks was inadequate or non-existent some banks followed very conservative reserve policies. Others, however, did not! An extreme example is provided by the Farmers' Exchange Bank of Gloucester (Rhode Island), founded in 1804. An investigating committee of the state legislature found that on the basis of only $3 million capital stock in gold, by 1809 the bank had loaned into circulation banknotes it had itself created to the total amount of $580 million.   In other words it had only sufficient reserves to liquidate about half a cent for every dollar of its obligations.[28]

It was the Civil War, however, which had the biggest impact on the system.   Once again gold was in short supply so the banks suspended payment making the issue of United States Notes [greenbacks] unavoidable.   Although the need was to meet the exigencies of war there had long been a need for a "universal" or national currency to replace the hodgepodge existing at the time.   One historian estimated that in 1860 there were "7,000 kinds of paper notes in circulation, not to mention 5,000 counterfeit issues."[29]

VICTORY OF THE BANKERS

From the time greenbacks first came into circulation in 1862 they carried the words: "The United States of America will pay to the bearer five dollars ... payable at the United States Treasury."   In fact, however, they were government-created inconvertible money until 1879 when they first became convertible into gold at face value. Convertibility was introduced by Hugh McCulloch, a former banker and gold monometallist who became secretary of the treasury in 1865. He agreed with his old buddies in the banking fraternity that steps should be taken to make greenbacks convertible into gold as soon as possible. Since there were hundreds of millions of dollars in paper outstanding at the time, and little gold in the treasury with which to redeem it, McCulloch concluded that it would be easier to reduce the number of greenbacks than to increase the gold in the treasury. So he sold bonds in exchange for greenbacks and then destroyed the greenbacks. In other words he exchanged interest-bearing debt for non-interest-bearing debt.[30] It is interesting to speculate what might have happened had McCulloch been a farmer or businessman. In any event, he decided to emulate mother England by putting the country in debt. There is little doubt that it was the bankers and moneylenders who won that round.

THE GOLD STANDARD - ANOTHER WRONG TURN

Of the three categories of monetary enthusiasts, those who preferred gold-backed currency, those who were quite willing to settle for silver-backed, and those who preferred no metal backing at all, it was ultimately the monometallists or gold standard supporters who carried the day. The gold standard was a commitment by participating countries to fix the prices of their domestic currencies in terms of a specific amount of gold - a practice followed in various European countries from time to time. "England adopted a de facto gold standard in 1717 ... and formally adopted the gold standard in 1819."[31] Convertibility was suspended during the Napoleonic War and re-instated in 1821, at the urging of economist David Ricardo, and others, at the pre-war rate of exchange.

"The United States, though formally on a bimetallic (gold and silver) standard switched to gold de facto in 1834 and de jure in 1900. Other major countries joined the gold standard in the 1870's. The period from 1880 to 1914 is known as the classical gold standard."[32] Eventually it became an international standard. It had to be abandoned during wartime as a matter of expediency. Later, when economic activity returned to normal, there was always pressure for its re-instatement.

The classical attachment to the gold standard was so strong that even the redoubtable Winston Churchill was captive of its orthodoxy. As Chancellor of the Exchequer, he was largely responsible for England's return to the gold standard at the old parity after World War I. In his Budget speech of April 28, 1925, he declared that: "A return to the gold standard has long been a settled and declared policy of this country. Every Expert Conference since the war ... has urged in principle the return to the gold standard. No responsible authority has advocated any other policy."[33]

Churchill stressed that in addition to those countries that had already returned to the gold standard there should be simultaneous action by Holland, the Dutch East Indies, Australia and New Zealand. Some other countries used U.S. dollars or British pounds as reserves on the basis that those currencies were convertible into gold and consequently they could be considered an acceptable substitute for gold. Churchill described the advantage of this common international action in the following metaphor: "That standard [the gold standard] may of course vary in itself from time to time, but the position of all countries related to it will vary together like ships in a harbour whose gangways are joined and who rise and fall together with the tide."[34]

Churchill based his case primarily on the Report of the Committee on the Currency and Bank of England Note Issues. The arguments of the Committee were brief and clear as far as they went, although they were described as jejune (devoid of substance) by J.M. Keynes. They never explored the general desirability of a gold standard from the point of view of the interests of the different social classes affected by its operation. The general advantages of a gold standard were not stated by the report, but were taken for granted as self-evident. So much for the opinions of "experts".

In retrospect one wonders why support for the gold standard was so deeply entrenched. It was obvious that every time gold went out of the country, to pay for imports, the money supply contracted and this had a negative effect on the domestic economy. On the other hand when gold was received in payment for exports the money supply increased rapidly and inflation took hold. This uncritical attachment to the gold standard must have had something to do with mysticism or its long romantic history as a prize worthy of kings and buccaneers. As an economic regulator, however, it was an abomination.

It is difficult for me to credit that such an absurd system would last until August 15, 1971, when President Richard Nixon announced that the United States would no longer redeem currency held by foreign central banks for gold. This action was the last gasp of the gold standard. It is even more difficult to believe, as Michael D. Bordo says in his essay on the Gold Standard in the *Encyclopedia of Economics*: "Widespread dissatisfaction with high inflation in the late seventies and early eighties brought renewed interest in the gold standard."[35] If true, and I am cynical enough to accept that it is, it only proves that some economists are incapable of learning.

To put the issue in perspective, just imagine that a group of visiting little green men and women from some other planet came to earth with a special laser gun which attacked only gold and caused it to disintegrate. In the course of their invasion they destroyed the entire gold supply on and in the earth. The effect on the real economy would be minimal. Jewellers would have to find substitutes for their brilliant wares and dentists would have to find something else to fill the gaping holes created in so many teeth. But apart from a few special cases, little would be affected. Our ability to grow food, in infinite variety, would not be changed. The potential for the production of bicycles, cars, ships and planes would not be affected. In other words we could cope quite nicely thank you. To say that without gold we would shut down the entire economy, or even slow it down dramatically, is too absurd for serious considera-tion. It should never have been the regulator of economic activity in industrialized economies.

It makes little difference to most of us how much gold our income will buy. What concerns us is the kind of "basket" of goods and services that Irving Fisher wrote about and which is now the basis for a consumer price index. How much food, clothing, and shelter will our pay-check buy and will there be anything left over for dinner out and family vacations? Also will it buy as much next year as it does now? And what about a few years from now, after we retire? These are the variables that we hope will be constant, on average, not how many gold or silver wafers we can buy with our dollars, pounds or marks. It is the package of goods and services that these currencies can be exchanged for which determines their value.

SUMMARY

To the question "What is money?", then, there is no single or simple answer. It has taken many forms over the centuries and new ones are being invented. Today most of the high quality coins of silver, gold and platinum are sold as collectors items. The day-to-day coins are usually alloys and, although they still form an essential part of the system, they really fall into the "small change" category. The fraction of the total value of transactions settled with coins is infinitesimal.

Paper money, or electronic impulses, now rule the day. We have gone through a history of paper money that was convertible, at least in theory, into gold; paper that was "backed" by silver; paper that was backed by other paper allegedly convertible into gold; and paper labeled "legal tender" backed by the authority of the state. In the final analysis money is anything that ordinary people will readily exchange for their goods and services. That is not the end of the story, however, it is really just the beginning.

One of the most important lessons from history is that when the money supply is increased faster than the output of goods and services, prices rise. Too much money causes inflation and it doesn't matter whether it's gold-backed money, government-created money, or bank-created non-convertible money. As J.K. Galbraith points out in his book *Money, Whence it Came, Where it Went,* one of the worst inflations Europe saw was when gold and silver were imported in large quantities from the Americas.[36]

On the other side of the coin it is obvious that too little money has, historically, led to economic stagnation. Whenever the money supply was contracted, the economy grew at a rate below its potential or, in many cases, shrank. So money is more than just a determinant of prices as some monetarists claim. A shortage of purchasing power, or aggregate demand as the economists call it, such as we saw during the great depression of the 1930's, and again in the two most recent and terrible recessions, slows an economy well below its potential, with the unhappy and sometimes tragic consequences which inevitably follow for individuals and families.

Finally, and fundamentally, it makes a profound difference how money is created. Government-created money is born free of encumbrance. <u>Bank-created money is slave money in the sense that it is brought into the world with a lien on it</u>. When the proportion of money created as debt is too great we find ourselves in the kind of Catch-22 we now face. To pay the interest on all that debt we have to borrow more and more all the time which is comparable to being in a deep hole and digging ourselves in deeper all the time.

CHAPTER 3

PHONY MONEY REIGNS SUPREME

"This is a pretty flim-flam."

Francis Beaumont and John Fletcher

Professor Joseph E. Stiglitz has written that banks "can be viewed as highly leveraged firms that borrow from depositors."[1] You better believe it – much too highly leveraged for the public good. Another definition which gives a better idea of what they actually do is: "banks are firms that borrow, lend, store, manufacture and destroy money." These are their principal functions although they are increasingly engaged in a number of other businesses where the legitimacy of their presence is open to question. It is their ability to create and destroy money, however, which provides the world's greatest economic challenge.

Those participants in the unofficial poll mentioned in the previous chapter who were willing to hazard a guess as to "where money comes from" invariably said, after some reflection, "the government prints it". When asked pointedly what proportion of new money they thought was printed by government the estimates ranged from 60 percent to 100 percent.   There were no guesses below 60 percent which, for me, confirmed the belief that money and banking constitutes the greatest void in public understanding of how our economic system works and why it sometimes works less well than we would like.   Governments, or central banks on their behalf, only print a small fraction of the total money supply, or money stock as it is often called.   At the end of 1992 it was about 8% of the total.   The vast majority of new money is created by private banks licensed for that purpose.

MULTIPLE CREATION OF MONEY BY THE BANKING SYSTEM

A simplified version of the process goes something like this.   When the Federal Reserve System (Fed) decides to increase the money stock it buys some government bonds, let's say a million dollars worth for purposes of illustration.   It pays for them by issuing a check for a million dollars drawn on itself.   This is the equivalent of cash and economists call it "high-powered money" because it is the kind of money banks can use as reserves in order to create a much larger amount of "deposit money".   When we were on the gold standard, gold was considered high-powered money.   Today, high-powered money consists of (1) paper money (cash) with "legal tender" printed on it and (2) banks' deposits at the Fed.

Let's assume that the entire million of new cash winds up in the banking system, i.e. in bank vaults or in the banks' deposits with the Fed.   They are then in a position to make new loans equal to several times the amount of fresh cash. Economist Anna J. Schwartz describes the process this way.

"If the required reserve ratio is 20 percent, then starting with new reserves of, say, $1,000, the most a bank can lend is $800, since it must keep $200 as reserves against the deposit it simultaneously sets up.   When the borrower writes a check against this amount in his bank A, the payee deposits it in his bank B.   Each new demand deposit that a bank receives creates an equal amount of new reserves.   Bank B will now have additional reserves of $800 of which it must keep $160 in reserves, so it can lend out only $640. The total of new loans granted by the banking system as a whole in this example will be five times the initial amount of excess reserve, or $4,000: 800 + 640 + 512.40 + 409.60, and so on."[2]

I think it is simpler for most of us to understand the phenomenon of bank-created money when we consider how many of us as individuals have been, or might be in the future, involved in the money-creation process. Let's assume that you would like to borrow $20,000 to buy a car or perhaps a new machine to make widgets in the basement. A visit to your friendly banker will set the ground rules. You will be told that you will have to provide collateral. If you have a drawer-full of stocks and bonds with market value well in excess of the amount to be borrowed that will probably be acceptable. If not, a mortgage on your house, assuming you have sufficient equity, may do. Failing that the personal guarantees of a couple of rich uncles or aunts might suffice.

Once the collateral has been agreed and deposited with the bank for safe-keeping, you will be asked to open an account and sign a note for the amount to be borrowed. Minutes later the bank will put $20,000 in your account and you can write a check any time you like. The important point is that just minutes earlier the $20,000 you have to spend didn't exist. It was created out of thin air based on nothing more than a small fractional reserve held by the bank.

An important point should be kept in mind, however. Although the bank "created" the $20,000 that was put in your account as a deposit this "phony money" – or money equivalent as it's sometimes called – was created as debt. You still owe the bank $20,000 and you won't get your collateral back until you repay the loan in full with interest.

An even more striking illustration of how the system of new money-creation works is to consider someone in the building business who borrows $150,000 to build a house. This money is used to pay the people who dig clay from a pit and make bricks, the bricklayers who lay the bricks, the woodsmen who cut trees to make lumber, the carpenters who use it to build the frame, the miners who extract the metals for the hardware and the manufacturers who turn out the plumbing, wiring and fixtures. But when they are all finished it is the bank which owns the house. The bank did little more than create the "money" which acted as the intermediary to facilitate construction. Nevertheless, because it was created as debt, all of the money used to pay for the new house had a lien on it. Consequently the builder has to sell the house at a price that will allow him to repay the bank and, if he is lucky, leave a little over to reward him for the work he has done and the risk he has taken. If he can't, and there is a shortfall, he will have to make up the difference to prevent the bank from liquidating part or all of the collateral pledged to get the loan.

In reality, then, the banks have turned the world into one humongous pawn shop. You hock your stocks, bonds, house, business, rich mother-in-law or country and the bank(s) will give you a loan based on the value of the collateral. Still there is an element of uncertainty in dealing with the banks that doesn't apply with legitimate pawn shops. The latter don't phone you and ask for their money back if the price of gold or silver goes down after they have given you cash for your gold watch or silver candlesticks. The banks, on the other hand, often change the terms of the deal with little warning. If the market value of your collateral goes down, they phone and insist that you either provide additional collateral, which you may not have, or give them their "money" back which isn't always easy if too many banks are simultaneously insisting on the repayment of too much "money" (in cash) which doesn't really exist. In the case of loans to countries, the banks can't really foreclose so they just begin to act like owners and tell the political managers how they want "their" country run.

Private banks are often referred to as financial intermediaries who take money from some people and lend it to others. It is a part truth but also part fiction when you consider that banks create more than 90% of the increase in the money stock each year in the form of debt and with less and less cash or reserves to back it up.

In view of this it was more than a little surprising that Anna J. Schwartz used a 20 percent reserve requirement in her

Encyclopedia of Economics example when there hasn't been a reserve that high in heaven knows when. You will recall that when the Bank of England was first chartered in 1694, it was only allowed to lend its capital twice. Then some collusion between bankers and politicians relaxed the reserve requirement. In the United States, for federally chartered banks, the reserve requirement was 25% in the late nineteenth century but this was reduced about the time the Fed was established and the slide has continued, periodically, ever since. On December 31, 1992 the Fed reserve requirement for Net transaction accounts (deposits against which you can make withdrawals or transfers) was 3 percent for the first 46.8 million and 10 percent for deposits in excess of that amount; 0 reserve was required against non-personal time deposits (savings); and 0 reserve against Eurocurrency liabilities.[3] The regulations are too complicated for mere mortals to understand but for anyone brave enough to try they are repeated in full in Appendix A. They are also too frightening for restful sleep. What they say to me is that the Fed and the banking system have jiggered definitions in a way that permits excessive leverage.

Figure 1 (see page 31) demonstrates the results of the manipulation. Whereas in 1963 there was one real dollar, or reasonable facsimile, for every ten dollars you had in the bank, that is no longer the case. Today you may have 25 to 30 dollars "in the bank" against which only one legal tender dollar exists. This is obscene. Greed knows no bounds!

Other countries' rules are as bad or worse. In Germany, the Bundesbank has current reserve requirements (May '94) of 5% on call loans and 2% on term deposits and savings accounts. In the United Kingdom, institutions which are members of the U.K. banking sector, and which have reported eligible liabilities (ELs) averaging 10 million pounds or more, accept an obligation to hold non-operational, non-interest-bearing deposits (cash ratio deposits) with the Bank of England. The level of an institution's cash ratio deposits is calculated twice a year, in April and October, as 0.35% of the average ELs reported. Compare that to the 50% when the Bank of England was first chartered as a private bank. In Canada

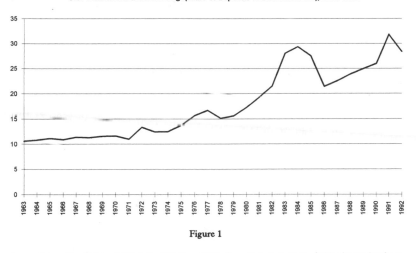

U.S. Commercial Bank Leverage(Ratio of Deposits to Bank Reserves), 1963-1992

Figure 1

Source: International Financial Statistics, IMF June 1993. Deposits include all checkable, time and savings deposits of commercial banks. The chart does not include money market instruments in the deposit numbers. If these MM instruments were included, bank leverage would be even greater.'

the Bank Act of 1991 provided, unbelievably, for the total elimination of reserves over a two year period – a move that, thankfully, the U.S. has resisted so far. Canadian banks just keep the minimum amount of cash they expect their customers to withdraw from day-to-day.

To understand the effect of the banking system on the real economy it may be useful to think of the money stock as soup. In some Eastern European countries, and also in some Third World countries where there is little to buy, the soup is mostly water. But in the highly developed Western economies our soup is rich with tasty morsels of meat and an endless variety of vegetables representing the incredible spectrum of goods and services that are available in such abundance. In other words, if you have cash you can satisfy almost any need or want.

Each year the soup is watered when the banking system increases the money stock. As long as they don't dilute it too much the system can produce the extra meat and vegetables to maintain the same rich tantalizing consistency. Either too much or too little can have negative effects on the brew. In real life the amount of dilution which will maintain the same consistency is determined by the potential to increase the supply of goods and services. This depends on the natural growth in the labor force, net immigration and participation rates (the proportion of the total population which chooses to work), as well as the level of education and skill of the total labor force, coupled with the use of more and better machines. For two centuries production has tended upward when monetary conditions, the means of exchange, has allowed.

WHO GETS THE LOANS

How the banks have been ladling out the increase in money for the last decade or so has put the world on notice that things are not as they used to be. This is a matter of concern because monetary dilution affects everybody from the poorest beggar with a cupful of change through to the multi-billionaire. In the real world some are treated much more generously than others and to a very large extent the banks decide who the winners and losers will be. Giving them a near-monopoly on the creation of money, and then allowing them almost unrestricted liberty as to what they can do with it, can best be described as double jeopardy. The banks may not have invented the maxim "the rich get rich and the poor get poorer" but they certainly do their best to prove its validity by giving the lion's share of the increase to their friends, beginning with themselves.

Get a breakdown, if you can, of the employee benefits hidden in the fine print within any bank annual statement and you will probably find a list of loans to executives for the purchase of homes or the acquisition of shares in the bank for which they have been given options. Often they get a preferred interest rate that makes even their best customers green with envy. They have another tremendous advantage in that when a loan comes due they can either renew it or give themselves large salary increases and bonuses sufficient to retire the loans.

If only everyone were in such a privileged position.

Other people who have access to increases in the money supply fall into the general category of "those who don't need it". They are well-to-do people with collateral assets who can borrow money from the banks, buy shares or property in anticipation of an increase in value, deduct the interest on the loan from their taxable income and make themselves a tidy profit if they have anticipated market conditions correctly. It's nice work if you can do it but only people with collateral assets are in a position to take advantage of the opportunity and they are the people who need it the least.

The banks are equally generous with their favorite large businesses and often invite the CEO to be a member of their board. That can make a difference. Two of my friends in the development business went to every Canadian bank in 1993 in an effort to borrow money for a large Vancouver development, with an assured future, in which they were investing 50 percent of the total cost from their own resources. No bank would look at the loan until a director of their company, who was also a bank director, interceded on their behalf and the loan was granted.

The trend in banking throughout the 1980's and into the 1990's is alarming. Small business has been devastated, while billions have been made available for takeovers and leveraged buyouts. The most credit-worthy borrowers kept raising the ante as they tapped the banking system for giant ladles of newly-created soup for the purpose of buying up other people's businesses. The banks loved it because it is so much easier to clip one coupon rather than worry about a thousand different collections – only one or two balance sheets to read rather than a drawer-full. Even then there were balance sheets that were not adequately checked when the borrower was a director of the bank.

The trend was summed up in the following quotation from John Ralston Saul's book, *Voltaire's Bastards*: "Capitalist creativity has been discouraged and financial manipulation encouraged. This starvation campaign has left the fat slightly thinner, having converted some of their flesh into cash. Now they are beefing themselves back up by picking over the carcasses of the young and lean. In 1984 alone, $140 billion was spent in the United States on mergers, acquisitions and leveraged buyouts. By 1988 this was almost $300 billion, with 3,310 companies involved.... The inevitable passing of the leveraged buyout as it first appeared does not represent a change in the situation, but rather the passing of a particular tool for speculation. For example, worldwide merger-acquisition transactions had risen to $375.9 billion in 1988, involving 5,634 deals. Then came the collapse in the speculative market. And yet the figures in 1989 were only marginally down, to $374.3 billion involving 5,222 deals."[5]

The number of questionable deals is staggering. One which was of particular interest to me was Robert Campeau's grandiose acquisitions. This was because I had known him as a builder and as a member of the Canadian *Task Force on Housing and Urban Development*, which I chaired. So, following his acquisition of Allied Stores, it was a matter of some amazement when he attempted to acquire Federated Department Stores' chain which comprised Bloomingdale's, Abraham & Strauss, Burdines, Lazarus, Rich's and Goldsmith's, amongst others. Actually I was more than somewhat dismayed because his expertise was in construction, where he had succeeded admirably; but he knew nothing about retailing, the amount of money involved was out of his league and I disapproved of anyone being able to borrow several billions to buy other people's businesses.

Still, as James Grant points out, "Campeau was able to borrow nearly the entire purchase price: $3.25 billion from a dozen banks, $2.1 billion from a trio of brokerage houses (First Boston, PaineWebber, and Dillon Read), in the shape of a 'bridge loan', and most of the $1.4 billion of 'equity'. Of the so-called equity, only $195 million was not borrowed. This hard core of equity, secured by the sale of an Allied Stores unit, Brooks Brothers, represented less than 3 percent of the purchase price. It was less than the $224 million in front-end fees that Campeau had agreed to pay to his banks."[6]

Looking at this and a number of more recent deals one is struck by the familiarity of the pattern. An overly ambitious borrower finds a greedy lender willing to put together a syndicate to finance the buyout. Big upfront fees are the sugar that baits the trap. You can be sure that some bankers exacted a handsome tribute when Viacom Inc. assembled the approximately $6.8 billion cash portion of its roughly $10 billion cash and stock merger with Paramount Communications Inc.[7] The Canadian banks' caper into the field of bloated communications takeovers followed hard on the heels of the giant Viacom deal. They passed the hat for Rogers Communications Inc.'s $2.15 billion takeover of Maclean Hunter Limited and, according to newspaper reports, the bankers were rewarded by up-front fees as high as $49 million.[8] It wasn't long before Rogers cable-TV subscribers were asked to fork out an extra $1 a month.[9] In the course of these ongoing monopoly games, usually using bank-created "debt" money, the whole system is being turned topsy-turvy. The net result is economic subversion.

THE GAMBLING BANKS

On June 16, 1994, at the invitation of the U.S. Consulate in Toronto, I had the privilege of attending a lunch-time seminar led by Howard Rosen, Executive Director of the U.S. Competitiveness Policy Council. Participants were shown slides indicating that U.S. competitiveness has suffered from inadequate investment in industry. The very low savings rate was cited as a matter of concern in this regard. When a slide was displayed which indicated the banks' collective investment in commercial real estate, however, it appeared that the problem has been not so much a shortage of funds as the way the banks have been allocating resources – both the savings that have been entrusted to their stewardship and the new money they have been creating. Far too much has been allocated to Third World bonds, commercial real estate and leveraged buyouts – which must be one of the most inflationary uses possible for bank-created money – leaving far too little for industrial expansion.

U.S. competitiveness has been eroded because the tremendous power accruing to banks, including their licenses to create money, has not been used responsibly in the public interest.

Apart from the unfairness, the shift to very large, as opposed to small, business loans has been an economic disaster. When banks lent a few thousand dollars or a million or two to a small business for either start-up or expansion purposes, new jobs were created. But when they began to lend hundreds of millions or billions for takeovers, jobs were extinguished. When corporations were acquired at inflated prices it was inevitable that costs had to be cut in order to service the enormous debt. To become lean and mean was the buzzword. That meant firing people – often people who had worked for a company for years or decades. Using either the public's savings or newly-created money in this way has been a total perversion of economic theory and previous economic practice. Stripped of all the rhetoric, the banks have been financing higher costs (inflation) and job displacement (unemployment) at the same time.

The banks' real estate loans became so irresponsible and attained such a high proportion of the total cost of development that the market went crazy. Values were inflated enormously and this contributed to the pressure to induce another recession. Governments were then left holding the bag. The banking system, led by the knights in shining armour at the Fed, began to contract the money supply and make life miserable for everyone. Interest rates rose, business slowed down, profits fell, government revenues declined and debts of governments soared.

INTERNATIONAL CONSEQUENCES

What banks do with their tremendous power to manufacture money obviously has international and global consequences of monumental proportions. Canadian banks, for instance, have often preferred to make loans to large American corporations wishing to buy up Canadian companies rather than to finance the development of Canada by Canadians. They prefer the triple A guarantees of the foreign borrowers and have gone out of their way to wine and dine them. Most takeovers of Canadian companies by foreigners, including Americans, were financed partially or wholly by Canadian banks. The Canadian banks were quite willing to use the savings of Canadians and the near monopoly they have over the creation of money in a way which was detrimental to the public interest. They were willing to sell an important part of Canadians' birthright in exchange for a few easy to manage loans.

Western banks, including both U.S. and Canadian banks, have been responsible for putting some of the poorest areas of the Third World into financial jeopardy. They went through a phase when it was chic, because it seemed like an easy way to make money, to lend large sums to Third World governments with few guarantees as to how the money would be spent. It may have been justice that some of the money wound up in Swiss banks and that the world's bankers were stuck with large write-downs of their highly questionable loans, but that isn't the end of the story.

Instead of the relatively rich western world providing financial support as an "engine for development" to the struggling two-thirds of the planet, we have, for more than a decade, been a net financial drain on the "wretched of the earth". As UNICEF shows in *The State of the World's Children 1992, Summary*, our protectionism costs the Third World some $55 billion a year in lost exports, which is more than the total aid they receive. Add the effects of protectionism to the weight of high cost loans and you have the international catastrophe that UNICEF reports.

"But it is, above all, the weight of past debts which threatens future progress ... the developing world owes approximately $1,300 billion to the governments and banks of the industrialized nations and to international financial institutions. Each year, the repayment of capital and interest amounts to approximately $150 billion - roughly three times as much as the developing world receives in aid. As it is impossible to meet these interest charges in full, the amount unpaid is added to the total debt owed ... When all transactions are taken into account – the net effect is that the developing world is now transferring $40 to $50 billion a year to the industrialized world."[10]

As the report indicates the emancipation of Africa is at stake.   ... "Debt is the new slavery that has shackled the African continent. Sub-Saharan Africa owes approximately $150 billion. Each year, it struggles to pay about one third of the interest which falls due; the rest is simply added to the rising mountain of debt under which the hopes of the subcontinent lie buried. The total inhumanity of what is now appearing is reflected in the single fact that even the small proportion of the interest which Africa does manage to pay is absorbing a quarter of all its export earnings and costing the continent, each year, more than its total spending on the health and education of its people. Ten years of prevarication over this problem has already damaged not only the Africa of today but the Africa of tomorrow. While more than $10 billion a year in interest repayments in being sluiced out of that desperately poor continent, tens of millions of children are losing their one opportunity to grow normally, to go to school and become literate, and to acquire the skills necessary for their own and their countries' development in the years to come."[11] From a Western economic stability perspective one must ask how realistically such loans are treated on banks' balance sheets.

You might think that following their experience with questionable loans to real estate developers, Third World governments and big highly-leveraged takeover schemes that banks would seek safe haven in a cycle of caution and conservatism. But that is not the case. Their penchant for gambling would appear to be congenital.

MORE BANK GAMBLING

Investing in bonds, for example, is considered to be conservative. If it is your own money, and there are unlikely to be circumstances requiring immediate liquidation, you can absorb a 10-20% loss in book value and just sit on the investment until it matures or until market conditions improve. Buying on margin, however, can put anyone at risk.

The risk was underlined in the *Wall Street Journal* of April 7, 1994. In an article entitled "Bond Market's Rout, The Worst Since 1987, Stuns Many Investors – Even Big, Savvy Players Get A Pounding as Leverage Proves to Be Dangerous – But Many Hold On and Wait" the *Journal* puts the situation in perspective. "To be sure, plenty of long-term bond investors aren't much concerned about the market's rout. Some own individual bonds and plan to hold them to maturity, thus avoiding any loss of capital.... The biggest losers, in contrast, may be the savvy players supposed to be smart enough to side-step market debacles. Hedge-fund operators such as Mr. [Michael] Steinhardt and Julian Robertson are reeling under losses, and big New York trading firms such as Goldman, Sachs & Co. and Bankers Trust New York Corp. are bruised."[12]

There appears to be no limit to the leverage financial institutions are willing to risk. Another article in the *Wall Street Journal* entitled "High Leverage at Kidder Could Lead to Headaches", by Laura Jereski, forecast some of the problems faced by its owner, General Electric Co., that have been reported subsequently.

"Kidder, Peabody Group Inc.'s massive inventory of securities makes it the most highly leveraged firm on Wall Street. And that could present a huge headache amid growing signs of distress in the mortgage-backed securities market.

"About one third, or $23 billion, of the overall $73 billion in assets the General Electric Co. unit held at year-end represent securities Kidder holds for its own account, according to regulatory filings. These positions could be more damaging to Kidder because any losses could go straight to its bottom line. Kidder has just $778 million in equity against those assets, the filings show. That means the firm has very little margin for error.

"Overall, Kidder held an astounding $94 in bonds, stocks and other assets for every $1 in equity as of year-end – making it the most highly leveraged firm on Wall Street.

Kidder holds about $12 billion in mortgage backed bonds alone, traders say. Kidder says it has trimmed that position this year, but won't say by how much."[13]

Another area in which banks gamble is foreign exchange. Not only do they put vast sums at risk, they build up a vested interest in monetary and exchange policies which may or may not be in their home country's interest. Holding sufficient reserves of foreign currencies to service their customers is both acceptable and desirable. When they start betting on currency markets, however, they add one more wild card to the banking game.

Of all the recent trends in banking the most alarming is the purchase and sale of derivatives. Just to read a brief lexicon of some of the different kinds of derivatives is enough to give one a bad headache. They include interest futures, interest options, currency futures, currency options, stock market index futures, options on stock market indices, interest rate swaps, currency and cross-currency interest rate swaps, just for starters. Some are so complicated that bank regulators themselves have a problem understanding them.

In the case of derivatives, too, there is a line between legitimate functions, such as hedging exchange rates for example, and pure gambling. Unfortunately the legitimate areas of swaps and options, designed to give buyers financial protection against adverse moves in such things as interest rates or foreign currencies, carry scant profits for the banks and securities firms that sell them. The big profits can only be realized from the exotic instruments as the *Wall Street Journal* reported in an article titled "Bankers Trust Thrives Pitching Derivatives, But Climate Is Shifting – Losses by Clients Like P&G May Crimp Plan to Move To Relationship Banking – Some Intense Pressure to Sell."[14]

"The appeal of such exotic instruments is that it takes a certain amount of expertise to craft them, so not every financial firm can compete. Further, they tend to be much more profitable for the seller. For example, the profit for the seller on a typical leveraged swap runs about eight times the level of a traditional interest-rate swap. The more complex and customized the product becomes, the higher the fees the bank can command.

"'Every bank of any size wants to sell [exotic derivatives] to a corporation,' says Christopher Sailer, treasurer of Brown-Forman Corp., a Louisville, Ky., distiller. 'They basically will promote it with whatever reasoning a treasurer will accept. They're there to generate transaction fees, and the way to do it is through sales.'"[15]

Derivatives in general and exotic derivatives in particular constitute two extremely worrisome trends. The first is a further estrangement between the paper and real economies. Instead of concentrating on the growth of the real economy, banks concentrate their ingenuity and energy in playing the paper game. To encourage non-bankers to gamble, rather than promoting their core businesses, only compounds the felony.

Equally alarming, the banks have not been willing, until very recently, to disclose the extent of their exposure. The numbers are astronomical. "To those who assume the worst", reports *The Banker*, in its February 1993 issue, "the banks' deep involvement in the $10 trillion derivatives markets 'is an accident waiting to happen'. Few industries have done more than banking in recent years to validate Murphy's First Law: anything that can go wrong, will go wrong. Could derivatives, one of the most rapidly expanding and complex areas of financial activity, prove Murphy right, yet again?"[16]

If you ask the people who are making money from this form of gambling, there is nothing to worry about. If you ask the regulators who might lose their jobs if anything does go wrong, you get reactions varying from nonchalance to near apoplexy. The recently retired Canadian Superintendent of Financial Institutions, Michael Mackenzie, indicated sufficient concern to issue guidelines for the banks but managed to confuse the issue before leaving office in the summer of 1994. "I am not in favour of over-reaction; I am not in favour of laying on a wider regulatory blanket over all this", Mr. Mackenzie told delegates to a conference on derivatives held in Toronto by the Canadian Institute. "But let's hope we do not have a major accident either in the United States or Canada where a significant-sized financial institution fails and it is related to a derivatives book. Because then the ball game will certainly change."[17]

Holy mackerel! That is tantamount to the Federal Aeronautics Administration saying we have looked at the new high-flying saucer, we think it will fly all right because the manufacturers and test-pilots say so; but if one should crash, and a lot of innocent people are hurt, we will certainly take a closer look. Fortunately, for all of us, Congressman Henry B. Gonzalez, Chairman of the House Committee on Banking Reform and Urban Affairs, is adopting a somewhat more skeptical position.

SUMMARY

From the end of the Korean War until the 1970's when anyone asked me if we could have another crash comparable to the early 1930's I said: "Impossible, we have learned so much from World War II and post-war experience, including demand management, that we will never allow anything that stupid again." I was wrong. The way things are going, anything could happen.

I find myself in complete agreement with economic journalist Robert J. Samuelson who ends his account of the Great Depression in the *Encyclopedia of Economics* this way. "Now it seems preventable. Then, it was baffling. World War I made restoration of the prewar economic system difficult, maybe impossible. But that is what world leaders attempted because it was all they knew and it had worked. Only its collapse convinced them to try something different. Old ideas were overtaken and overwhelmed. It has happened before – and could again."[18]

Indeed it could and probably will unless the banks are required to limit their gambling, increase their reserves, and change their priorities in order to bring the paper and real economies together in some sort of harmony.

CHAPTER 4

AN INFINITELY SILLY SYSTEM

"Taxation without representation is tyranny. "

James Otis

Can you imagine any congressman introducing a motion to this effect: "Be it resolved that the Congress of the United States hereby issues exclusive licences to chartered banks to manufacture all or nearly all of the new money put into circulation each year and to direct and divide it in accordance with their own best interests and those of their friends and close associates." Doesn't that strike you as silly? Yet that, in reality, is exactly what the Banking Act of 1935 did. It gave privately-owned chartered banks, regulated only by a federal reserve system owned by some of them, an exclusive mandate to manufacture or create money - apart from the small amount of treasury notes in circulation. Monetary sovereignty for the United States of America has been delegated to private banks.

The system is so silly that I really have difficulty knowing how to describe it. Normally I don't have too much difficulty coming up with appropriate adjectives. I've written five books previous to this one as well as bi-weekly columns for ten years for the *Toronto Sun* and its syndicate *Canada Wide Features*. So I have had considerable practice in digging for words but in this case, I found, nothing seemed adequate. Ridiculous, inane, insane, grotesque, absurd and other adjectives crossed my mind but in each case they failed to portray the enormity of the situation and the outrage that fills my mind when I think how perverse the system really is. Finally, one evening, as I was contemplating the stars and distant galaxies, the word infinite came to mind. That was it. Our present monetary system is an infinitely silly system.

Some things are ironic in the extreme – indeed quite incomprehensible. Why would the people of the United States fight a war to gain independence from England because, in part, the mother country wouldn't permit the colonies to print their own currency while insisting that they borrow from British banks instead,[1] win the war and subsequently adopt the monetary scam invented by the British goldsmiths? Especially when they had ingeniously experimented with an infinitely superior system.[2]

The fact that the British system, like measles, spread across the industrial world is one of the greatest tragedies of the two centuries since the industrial revolution began. Its spotty record of recurrent booms and busts has created untold heartache. Little wonder that there was an insistent cry for the establishment of central banks to regulate the excesses of the highly-leveraged, panic-prone, privately-owned banks. In the United States the Federal Reserve System was established in 1913, no doubt with high expectations. That these expectations have not been met is readily apparent to anyone who will take the time to read the record of recurrent crises.

For "light" reading on a holiday in March, 1994, I took along *A Monetary History of the United States 1867-1960*, the 800 plus page opus by Milton Friedman and Anna Jacobson Schwartz. Reading it is enough to make one cry – or to get very, very angry, depending on the mood of the moment. It chronicles the failure of the system to provide consistent and measured monetary growth proportionate to the potential for increased goods and services; the inability of the Fed to prevent widescale bank failures; and the near-total paralysis of the system when it came to addressing the needs of the real economy, especially during the Great Depression.

After the second banking crisis, in March, 1931, deepened the severity of the depression, President Hoover organized a nation-wide drive to assist private relief agencies in the Fall of that year. His committee of seventy was named the President's Unemployment Relief Organization. "The unemployed in many states formed self-help and barter organizations, with their own systems of scrip."[3] When the monetary system broke down the people, once again, as they had in earlier colonial days, invented their own money as a matter of necessity.

Will Rogers, the great American humorist and folk hero reported general agreement as to who was responsible for the monetary mess. On February 24, 1932, he warned that: "you can't get a room in Washington ... Every hotel is jammed to the doors with bankers from all over America to get their 'hand out' from the Reconstruction Finance Corporation ... And I have asked the following prominent men in America this question, 'What group have been more responsible for this financial mess, the farmers? ... Labor? ... Manufacturers? ... Tradesmen, or Who?' ... And every man - Henry Ford, Garner, Newt Baker, Borah, Curtis, and a real financier, Barney Baruch - without a moment's hesitation said, 'Why, the big bankers.' ... *Yet they have the honor of being the first group to go on the 'dole' in America!"*[4]

There may have been consensus as to who was responsible for the crisis but there was certainly no agreement on what to do about it. The contrasting attitudes of politicians, elected to serve the people, and the economic elite strikes a familiar chord.

"In Congress, however, there was growing support for increased government expenditures and for monetary expansion, proposals widely castigated by the business and financial community as 'greenbackism' and 'inflationary'. On its part, the business and financial community, and many outside it, regarded federal deficits as a major source of difficulty.

Pressure to balance the budget finally resulted in the enactment of a substantial tax rise in June 1932. The strength of that sentiment, which, in light of present-day views seems hard to credit, is demonstrated by the fact that in the Presidential campaign of 1932, both candidates ran on platforms of financial orthodoxy, promising to balance the federal budget."[5] Doesn't that sound like déjà vu?

When the Federal Reserve Banks closed their doors on March 4, 1933, "The central banking system, set up primarily to render impossible the restriction of payments by commercial banks, itself joined the commercial banks in a more widespread, complete, and economically disturbing restriction of payments than had ever been experienced in the history of the country. One can certainly sympathize with Hoover's comment about that episode: 'I concluded [the Reserve Board] was indeed a weak reed for a nation to lean on in time of trouble.'"[6] Not only has there been little change in attitude since the 1930's, it appears that little has been learned from the experience. Americans still put their trust in a system regulated by a Fed which gives the interests of the banks and the money-lenders a higher priority than the interests of the country.

To the North, the Bank of Canada wasn't established until 1935. Prior to its establishment there appears to have been the usual difference of opinion between the bankers and ordinary people as to what its role should be. This dichotomy was summed up in an article in *Maclean's Magazine* in the summer of 1933.

"The point which our bankers seem to miss is that what the Canadian people want in a central bank is not to supply the other banks with rediscount facilities which they already have or to save us from future panics, [as, it is previously noted, U.S. experience shows they do not] but they do want an institution that will effectually control the whole of the money and credit of the nation, now under the control of the other banks, and which will somehow be able to make that money and credit available in sufficient volume wherever legitimately needed, and on terms much more fair and equitable than at present."[7] It was a pious hope that has not yet been realized.

To give them a little credit the Fed, in the U.S., and the Bank of Canada, in Canada, did help facilitate the financial requirements of World War II. And even though they did allow more government-created money in wartime than they had before, or have since, they stubbornly maintained the myth that it is privately-owned banking corporations which are endowed with the primary responsibility to "print" money. In the process government bonds were allowed as reserves for the banks in both countries so that the money lent to government became the basis on which the banks could create even more money with which to buy more government bonds.

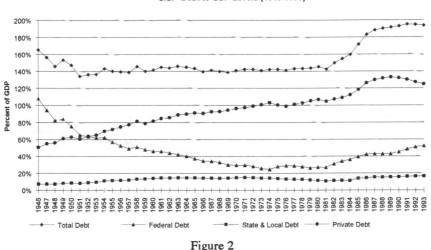

U.S. - Debt to GDP Levels (1946-1993)

Figure 2

Source: Flow of Funds Accounts Financial Assets and Liabilities Year End – Table L2 through L4, U.S. Federal Reserve System, Washington, D.C.

It was the two decades after the war, including the fifteen golden years from roughly 1950-1965, when the system seemed to have found its stride. Growth was solid, jobs were available for people who wanted to work, inflation was modest, demand management was accepted as a legitimate concept and everyone seemed reasonably content with the economics profession. The ratio of total debt to GDP in the United States fell from slightly above 165%, in 1946, to a low of 134%, in 1951, and then remained more or less constant in the 135-145% range for 30 years until 1981. During the same period Federal government debt declined from a high of about 107% of GDP in 1946, to a low just under 25% in 1974, and then hovered in the 26-29% range until 1982 (See Figure 2).[8] As you can see, the reduction in federal debt was achieved at the expense of a corresponding increase in private debt.

A STUPID RECESSION 1981-82

If the first quarter-century after World War II moved along comparatively smoothly the same cannot be said for the second quarter-century. A dramatic change occurred which is not sustainable in the long run.

We are told that beginning sometime during the 1970's "Central bankers in leading countries, including the United States, no longer offer a laundry list of important objectives. They now most often describe their principal task as the maintenance of price stability."[9] That is interesting information! Who made the decision? Congress? Parliament? I know dozens of politicians in several countries and I cannot recall a single conversation in which one of them said: "Guess what? We have decided to concentrate on inflation and forget about unemployment." Perhaps I wasn't listening, but as one familiar with how the system works I would guess that this decision was taken by bureaucrats and bankers – people who normally can survive a recession without losing their jobs. They would then "advise" governments overly dependent on their advice.

In any event, that's how the cookie crumbled. At the outset of the 80's Fed Chairman Paul Volcker in the U.S., and his opposite numbers in several other countries, decided to give their economies a good thrashing. Apparently Volcker and his opposite numbers had not learned from the 1970 and 1975 recessions that monetarily-induced reductions in inflation rates were only temporary. Instead they must have concluded that the failure of those earlier tests could be attributed to a lack of will.   The contractions hadn't been sufficiently long or sufficiently severe. So, steeped in the monetarist theology, they decided to carry the 1981-82 experiment to its logical conclusion – presumably zero inflation. Before reaching that target, however, it became obvious that they might succeed in collapsing the whole Western monetary system.   Either prudence or fright caused them to turn off their death machines just in time to prevent a catastrophe.

Just as most people are not really aware of how banks create money, by creating deposits, they are equally unfamiliar with the opposite action. Banks destroy money (credit) when they call loans. The Fed decides to sell a bond for cash or its equivalent. The amount of high-powered money outstanding is reduced by the amount of the transaction. This requires the banks to reduce the loans outstanding by an equivalent amount multiplied by their leverage. It is a chain reaction. When the system is expanding, it is like a balloon. When it is contracting the system acts like a balloon with a pin stuck in it, i.e. a recession or depression.

I know that someone will argue, as the President's Council of Economic Advisers did in February 1983, that the very sharp decline in 1982 did not reflect a decrease in the growth of the monetary aggregates. "Rather the exceptional severity of the slowdown in nominal GNP growth can be traced to a combination of factors that led to an unusually sharp decline in the velocity of money, that is, in the ratio of GNP to the money stock."[10]

What did they expect? Faced with staggering unemployment, people with jobs decided it was prudent to hang on to their money in case their pink slip was next. So for a number of reasons, including fear and uncertainty of the future, the velocity of money declined and the U.S. sank into the deepest recession in fifty years. As always, it was the poor who suffered most. As Isabel V. Sawhill wrote in her essay on "Poverty in the United States" for the *Encyclopedia of Economics*: "Researchers have found that recessions have a disproportionate impact on the poor because they cause rising unemployment, a reduction in work hours, and the stagnation of family incomes. The link between macroeconomic conditions and the incidence of poverty was clearly visible during the 1982 recession, when the poverty rate rose to 15.2 percent, up from 13.0 percent in 1980."[11]

The callous attitude of the Fed and other central banks was, in a sense, legitimized by the notion of a natural rate of unemployment defined as the lowest rate of unemployment tolerable without pushing up inflation. This idea, advanced by Milton Friedman and Edmund Phelps, has been a great disservice to both economic theory and performance. Specifically it has directed attention away from an attempt to find the reasons for the increased inflation that began in the mid-60's by making an unnatural situation sound normal instead of abnormal.

I recall addressing a class of university students some years ago on the subject of contemporary inflation and telling them how a common sense incomes policy would wrestle it to the ground. In the question period that followed a young man rose, and with that combination of brashness, irreverence and sarcasm of which I might have been guilty at the same age, asked if I had not heard of the "natural rate of unemployment?" I was not sure that I had because it was just a new invention – an excuse to cover the economists' lack of understanding of the origin of stagflation.

In an interview with Nobel laureate Gunnar Myrdal, who claimed credit for coining the word stagflation, he admitted that he didn't understand what caused it. My thesis, which will be elaborated in a later chapter, is that stagflation resulted from the irresponsible use of monopoly power on the part of big labor and big business. Wage settlements were negotiated that were well in excess of productivity increases. Labor unit costs rose, followed by prices. Central banks were put in the invidious position of having to print enough money to clear the market at the new higher price levels, which would bring roaring inflation, or of refusing to finance the process which would produce massive unemployment. In practice most of them compromised, resulting in too much inflation and too much unemployment at the same time – hence "stagflation".

Inventing a "natural rate" of unemployment, about which there is nothing natural at all, was an attempt to rationalize the phenomenon.   In the process it became a license for central banks to pursue inhumane and irrational policies.

Just step back a pace or two and take a clear look at what they did.   In 1981-82 the Fed in the U.S., and central banks in other countries, deliberately put millions of people out of work.   The ranks of the unemployed swelled to 30 million in the Western world.   Then governments everywhere began to scramble around and introduce new programs of every type and description to try to re-employ a few of them.   Can you imagine anything more brilliantly insane than one arm of government extinguishing millions of jobs while other arms, at considerable cost to taxpayers, try to create a few thousands to fill the void?   It is comparable to deliberately torpedoing a ship-load of passengers and then sending a few lifeboats to rescue a minority of the stragglers.

A SECOND STUPID RECESSION

We hadn't fully recovered from the effects of the 1981-82 recession when the spin doctors who control our destiny decided to give us another massive injection of their pain producer.   We were told, of course, that it would just be short-term pain necessary to restore the economy to full health – to "re-establish the fundamentals", as they call it.

Why, when they have used the same medicine at least half a dozen times in the course of the last forty years and the fundamentals aren't right yet, would anyone believe them?   Especially why would politicians believe them?   When a Liberal government allowed the Bank of Canada to sabotage the Canadian economy in 1981-82 the Progressive Conservative opposition finance critic, Mike Wilson, is alleged to have said: "This is insane."   A decade later, as Minister of Finance, the same Wilson defended the Bank's repeat performance - even more ruinous than the one he had labeled as "insane".

In reality, politicians have become little more than talking heads. In opposition they criticize, often with much justice, the financial policies of the government. Then the sides change and the roles reverse. It is a phenomenon I understand only too well from personal experience. The so-called "expert" advisers get politicians in closed rooms and brief them fervently. They call the meetings "information briefings" but often the real object of the exercise is intimidation. Their purpose is to persuade the politicians that their natural instincts are wrong and that the experts are right and that non-compliance could lead to some financial disaster for which "you, Mr. Secretary" or "you, Minister" would be held responsible. It is difficult, bordering on impossible, to stand up to that kind of pressure. Instead, most politicians get stuck with accepting the consequences of taking advice from experts who, all too often, are the kind of experts who have all the answers without necessarily being familiar with the problems. The tragedy of the last fifteen to twenty years is that the consequences of official advice have rendered politicians impotent to cope with people's real problems and this has undermined confidence in the efficacy of the political system and, of course, of politicians themselves.

The fallout from what I consider bad advice has been enormous. While discussion of the disadvantages for the poor and those who lose their jobs has been widespread, less has been said about the side effects on business and government. Each recession produces a fresh wave of bankruptcies and many of the victims are innocents who would have no way of knowing that an unexpected restriction or reduction in their line of credit, at a critical juncture of their development, could turn their dreams into a nightmare of insolvency. Figure 3 illustrates the increase in losses due to bankruptcies beginning with the 81-82 recession.

Even less talked about are the effects of high interest rates on those businesses that weather the storm. Higher interest rates increase costs and cut into profits in an environment where it's difficult to raise prices enough to cover the increased tribute to the money lenders. Figure 4 shows that while non-financial corporate profits before-interest-payments have remained reasonably constant from 1952 to 1988, the after-interest-payment profits have fallen by half from about 10% of GDP to approximately 5% with the steepest decline occurring in the early 1980's when the Fed pushed interest rates through the roof.

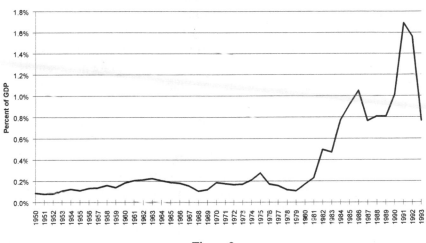

Figure 3

Source: Economic Report of the President, Table B-95, 1994

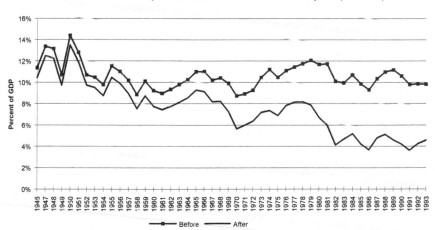

Figure 4

Source: National Income and Product Accounts, Tables 1.1, 1.16, 8.8

The effects of the high interest rates inflicted on an unsuspecting public in 1981-82, and to a lesser degree since, are far-reaching and long term. When people lose their jobs they don't pay income tax. Instead they look to government for help. When businesses go bankrupt, or if their profits are squeezed, they pay less corporation tax. This includes profits reduced by higher interest charges.

All of this pain flows through to governments which are, without doubt, the biggest "corporate" losers. Two things happen. As soon as a recession strikes, government revenues fall. Bigger deficits are the inevitable result. When these deficits translate into debt, which debt is then compounded at higher and higher interest rates, the debt to output (GDP) ratio starts to skyrocket.

A couple of years ago I bumped into a retired central banker on the subway platform. Not surprisingly the discussion turned to the "financial mess". His position was clear and straightforward. All our ills could be traced to the profligacy of governments. At that point I suggested that perhaps we should change the subject. I am not an apologist for government spending that is either extravagant or stupid, and there is much of both. That is the story which fuels cocktail conversation and editorial indignation. But the big story, which is seldom written or talked about, is that the last two recessions have given government finances a giant kick in the pants from which it will be difficult to recover.

My central banker friend understood so little of politics and life that he thought you should be able to cut government expenses by 10% in the few months it took to crush the life out of the economy. But that isn't in the nature of how governments work. They are not like private corporations and they can't just send out thousands of pink slips and slash social programs and defence spending overnight. Nor can governments default on the huge cost of servicing the national debt. They can't present a plan for re-structuring when they feel the ground going soft beneath them. About the best they can do is try to hold the line and hope for better times to come.

In the meantime debt to income levels start to rise. If you refer back to Figure 2 you will note that the U.S. federal debt to income ratio fell from a high of over 107% in 1946 to a low of about 25% in 1974. This was made possible by a combination of factors including a reasonable rate of growth and, in the early post-war years, very low interest rates. A reduction in federal debt was accommodated in the system by a corresponding increase in private debt so that the total debt to income level remained more or less constant from 1951 to. 1981. That's when the explosion occurred. The recession and post-recession policies not only facilitated the biggest transfer of wealth from poor to rich in history, it marked the beginning of a very substantial rise in both federal and total debt compared to income.

In *A Matter of Interest*, Wm. Hixson estimates that should the interest on debt continue to increase at the rate it did from 1947 to 1987 in 40 years, by 2027, total debt interest would be 100% of national income. He underlines the fact that this is not a prediction because it is an impossibility. "It does, however, amount to a prediction that the way the economy is structured and the way it functions will have to be drastically modified sometime in the not too distant future."[12] The increasing interest burden is mathematically unsustainable in the long run which is not too surprising for an infinitely silly system.

AN EVEN MORE FOOLISH REGRESSION

It should be obvious from glancing at the data that any reprise of the post-World War II improvement in the federal debt to GDP will require strong growth and low interest rates, i.e. federal borrowing rates lower than the growth rate if the existing debt is to be accommodated without further increases in taxes. So what does the Fed, led by Chairman Alan Greenspan do? After just a few weeks of robust growth the screws are turned, interest rates increased, and the rate of growth slowed when there is still some slack in the economy and involuntary unemployment, which is not "natural", remains at a morally unacceptable rate for a civilized country.

Not only that, the Fed's 1994 increases in interest rates played havoc with markets both in the U.S. and elsewhere. Stocks and bonds plummeted. In Canada, where there had not yet been anything like robust growth, interest rates rose to put a further damper on a recovery that could only be described as fragile, at best. The question arises as to whether central bankers in their blind pursuit of hard money really have any idea what they are doing to real economies and real governments? Does it make sense to raise interest rates, increase the cost of servicing government debt, and put additional strain on deficits?

First, the central bankers, with the private banks cheering them on, induced the recessions that put governments deeper and deeper in debt and made it almost impossible for them to balance their budgets. Then senior bank officials start making speeches about how the country should be run. Governments should raise taxes, but not in the area of financial transactions where there is a lot of loose change to be found. They should cut programs. They shouldn't spend more money on infrastructure, housing or health care because, if they do, markets will add a premium to the rate they charge on the "money" they lend to them.

It is my strong conviction that private banks should not have been given the power to manufacture money to lend to federal governments at interest. This is a gift which the banks did nothing to earn. Worse, it is a form of taxation. When banks lend newly-created money to governments (the people) they are guaranteed that the government will tax the people in order to repay both principal and interest. Isn't that unconstitutional? You even have private banks in other countries creating money to convert into U.S. currency for the purpose of buying U.S. government bonds. Is there no limit to the scam?

When you survey the damage wrought by central bankers, who act as if they are accountable to no one, you wonder about the "leaders", especially economists, who want to entrench that despotic power. The most powerful economic weapon in the entire arsenal is to be entrusted to someone at arms length from responsibility? Marriner Eccles may have been a "smart cookie", as one of my friends describes him, but only a banker would have advised Franklin D. Roosevelt to establish a seven-man Federal Reserve Board at arms length to the Treasury.

In Canada and the United Kingdom governments have retained ultimate responsibility in theory, at least, if not in practice. But there are advocates of a completely independent central bank modelled on the Bundesbank. If I were someone living in the European community I would live in fear and dread of a single currency in the hands of bankers trained in that school. The interests of the usurers would take preference over all other human interests. The paper economy would prevail.

The worst and most frightening of competing ideas on monetary reform comes from Harvard economist and former Under Secretary for Economic Affairs, Richard N. Cooper. In a paper entitled "A Monetary System for the Future" he proposes the creation of a common currency for all the major western industrailized countries with a common monetary policy and a joint Bank of Issue.[13] The Bank of Issue, with overall responsibility for determining monetary policy, would be governed by a board made up of representatives of national governments whose votes would be weighted according to the share of their country's gross national product to the total GNP of the community of participating nations.

A principal purpose of the proposed "reform" would be to reduce the fluctuations in real exchange rates which is another way of saying that the interests of citizens of individual countries must be subordinate, in the future, as they often have been in the past, to the interests of international finance. National governments might exercise some influence with their own nominee, in theory, but in fact they would no longer be able to pursue any kind of independent monetary policy. Sovereignty over the most powerful of all economic tools would be turned over to an international monetary monster.

A world bank run by a world kingship of international appointees collectively not accountable to anyone? Heavenly days! Has the man of letters never heard of the Magna Carta? And what about the American War for Independence to free these United States from taxation without representation?

Allons enfants de la patrie, le jour de gloire est arrivé. Where are the farmers with their pitchforks? Where are the workers with their baseball bats and shotguns? It's time for another revolution! But this time a revolution of the mind!

CHAPTER 5

NOTHING NEW UNDER THE SUN

"All great truths begin as blasphemies."

George Bernard Shaw

I was somewhat astonished to learn a couple of years ago that Nobel laureate Milton Friedman has long been an advocate of monetary reform. He had been associated in my mind with two theories, monetarism and a "natural rate" of unemployment, which, in their application to the real economy, I consider to be the two most unfortunate ideas to come on the economic stage since the Great Depression. It was with surprise and pleasure, then, that I found his name amongst the handful of pioneers who advocate an end to the fractional reserve system of banking and the substitution of a 100 percent reserve system.

First in an article entitled "A Monetary and Fiscal Framework for Economic Stability" published in the *American Economic Review*, in 1948,[1] and later in *A Program for Monetary Stability*, published in 1959,[2] Friedman makes the case for fundamental change. In the book he wrote: "As a student of Henry Simons and Lloyd Mints, I am naturally inclined to take the fractional reserve character of our commercial banking system as the focal point in a discussion of banking reform. I shall follow them also in recommending that the present system be replaced by one in which 100% reserves are required."[3]

I was even more surprised to learn that the economist whose work had influenced me the most at university, Irving Fisher, had also recommended a 100% reserve system of banking. It was his theory of money which first convinced me that recessions and depressions were monetary phenomena and, by extension, totally unnecessary. Not until the winter of 1993, when I began the research for this book, did I become aware of his *100% Money*[4] and took the opportunity to read it. A man whose advice, had it been taken, would have helped us escape the worst ravages of the Great Depression, Fisher deserves a place high on the list of the great economists of all time.

Of course the idea of substituting government-created money for bank-created money was not original with these men despite the A+ they deserve for recognizing the merit of the concept. As we saw in Chapter 2, the American colonies had conducted experiments with government-created money as an alternative to borrowing from British banks. In Pennsylvania, for example, within a few years after it began to put paper money into circulation, with mortgaged real estate as security, a remarkable revival of its economy took place. It was reported that in Philadelphia in 1726, twice the number of ships were built as in any year previously.[5]

LINCOLN AND GOVERNMENT-CREATED MONEY

Although Abraham Lincoln was not a proponent of government-created money, he certainly recognized its usefulness in time of emergency. In his December 1862 message to Congress, Lincoln made the following reference to greenbacks: "The suspension of specie payments by banks soon after the commencement of your last session, made large issues of United States Notes [greenbacks] unavoidable. In no other way could the payment of the troops, and the satisfaction of other just demands, be so economically or so well provided for. The judicious legislation of Congress, securing the receivability of these notes for loans and internal duties, and making them a legal tender for other debts, has made them a universal currency; and has satisfied, partially, at least, and for the time, the long-felt want of an uniform circulating medium, saving thereby to the people immense sums in discounts and exchanges."[6]

There was some Congressional support for adopting the system on a permanent basis. Representative Thaddeus Stevens, first elected to Congress as a Whig and later as a Republican, in speaking during the spirited debates over the first of the Legal Tender Acts, prior to the enactment of the legislation authorizing the printing of greenbacks,[7] said: "The government and not the banks should have the profit from creating a medium of exchange."[8]   Another booster was Alexander Campbell, a mining engineer and entrepreneur, elected to Congress from Illinois in 1874 for a single term on a Democrat-Independent ticket. In *The True Greenback* he wrote: "The war has resulted in the complete overthrow and utter extinction of chattle slavery on this continent, but it has not destroyed the principle of oppression and wrong. The old pro-slaver serpent, beaten in the South, crawled up North and put on anti-slavery clothes and established his headquarters in Wall Street where ... he now, through bank monopolies and non-taxed bonds, rules the nation more despotically than under the old regime. ... I assert ... that an investment of a million dollars under the National Banking Law, or in non-taxed government securities, will yield a larger net income to its owner than a like amount invested in land and slaves employed in raising cotton and sugar did in the South in the palmiest days of the oligarchy."[9]

It was the bankers' view which carried the day, however.   In March, 1865, President Lincoln appointed a banker, Hugh McCulloch, secretary of the treasury. In a speech at Ft. Wayne, Indiana, in 1868 McCulloch said: "I look upon an irredeemable paper currency as an evil.... Gold and silver are the only true measures of value. I have myself no more doubt that these metals were prepared by the Almighty for this very purpose."[10]

Of course McCulloch's view of the Almighty did not end the controversy. Farmers, in particular, kept it alive. As grain prices fluctuated precariously, they became increasingly infuriated at what they considered to be usurious interest rates demanded by the banks, and government largesse toward the railroads. "The government had given four western railroads as much land as Ohio, Indiana, Michigan, and Wisconsin together, in addition to millions of dollars in loans or outright subsidies."[11] The farmers' acute unhappiness led to a kind of populism which embraced both the nationalization of money-creation and of the railroads. The platform of the People's Party of America in 1892, for example, called for "a national currency, safe, sound, and flexible, issued by the General Government only, a full legal tender for all debts, public and private, and this without the use of banking corporations.... the government to own and operate the railroads in the interest of the people."[12] Despite the valiant efforts of the dissenters, the bankers' orthodoxy prevailed.

CANADA AND SOCIAL CREDIT

Canadian opinion, as is often the case, parallelled that south of the border. Western farmers nursed the same two pet hates - the banks and the railroads. The boiling point came during the Great Depression when western unrest spawned new populist political parties including one called Social Credit, based primarily on the concept of monetary reform. It began as a provincial party which formed a government in Alberta, in 1935, where it tried to put its beliefs into practice. The Supreme Court of Canada ruled the attempt unconstitutional because money and banking were the exclusive responsibility of the federal government.

Undeterred, the Social Crediters formed a federal party and elected a strong block of MPs who were already in Ottawa when I became a neophyte member in 1949. Their leader was Solon E. Low, an articulate Albertan backed by others including Victor Quelch, MP for Acadia, and probably the most respected of the theorists, and John Blackmore, a Mormon priest who hammered away at the subject so consistently that there was a time when I could have repeated his remarks almost verbatim from memory.

Solon Low spoke for his party in criticizing the existing system. "Let us for a moment take a look at the financial and money system of these fellows who run the government", he said. "They believe that before we can add to the national wealth we must go out to the money brokers and borrow enough to complete or develop any one of our national resources and then pay interest to the money brokers for the use of our own money. We Canadians, therefore, are compelled to add to the national debt every time we wish to add to the national wealth. They call that sensible - the very people who ignorantly refer to social credit as funny money!"[13]

The substance of their concern can be summed up in two brief quotes. The first from John Blackmore, "What Social Crediters have advocated is to create enough money and to put it into circulation in the right places to enable the purchasing power of the people to equal the amount of goods on sale on the market."[14] The second, as expressed by a subsequent leader of the party, Robert Thompson, is the one that kept ringing in my ears: "Our aim is to make financially possible what is physically possible."[15] In effect Thompson was proposing a marriage of the physical and paper economies.

The Social Credit party, and its predecessor the Social Credit League, had been inspired, at least in part, by the writings of Major C.H. Douglas, a British engineer who, like a lot of ordinary people, gifted with a certain amount of common sense, had observed the periodic shortage of purchasing power in the British economy. To explain his position, Major Douglas employed his celebrated "A + B" theorem, in which he divided all costs of production into two categories. The "A" costs included all payments that producers (factories) made to individuals, such as wages, salaries and dividends, the "B" costs included all payments made to organizations for such things as raw materials, machinery, maintenance of plant, bank charges, etc. Thus, for any period, the total costs of production were represented by A + B, but the amount of money available to purchase the output of the period was only A, because B costs were largely in the nature of business "reserves", mere bookkeeping items which, while included in total costs of production, did not represent income distributed.[16]

The theorem was an abstraction with absurd implications and consequently was ripped to shreds by the classical economists.   Some of the things that Douglas identified, however, were perfectly valid.   The periodic shortage of purchasing power, for example, would later be acknowledged by Keynes.   In this respect both men questioned the validity of Say's law which had been such an impediment to the development of economic thought.   Say's law was incorrect when it suggested that all production creates an equal and opposite demand.   It obviously hadn't and to pretend otherwise was a stumbling block of monumental proportions.   A fundamental difference in principle between Douglas and Keynes, who lumped the engineer in with Marx as "underworld figures",[17] was in their method of filling the purchasing gap. Douglas would use government-created money – too much as he proposed it – while Keynes would have governments borrow their way to prosperity in the belief that eventually equilibrium would be restored and the extra debt would be repaid.

The A + B theorem didn't make sense.   But one could easily conclude that there were problems involved in trying to borrow your way to prosperity and that somehow the gap between the purchasing power available and the amount required to clear the market had to be filled.   This was the missing link that my professors could never come up with at university.   They knew the gap existed; they knew that there was a periodic shortage of purchasing power even if they couldn't or wouldn't explain why; but they had no suggestions when it came to a mechanism for equating demand with supply in the long run.   It was a subject which you couldn't talk about because most people didn't understand it and those who had been trained in economics were too impatient to listen.

DEBT-FREE MONEY RESURFACES

There have been few public proponents of the concept of debt-free money for many years until recently when the idea resurfaced.   One spokesman is a bright and very articulate young Canadian, Jordan Grant, president of Seaton Group and chairman of the Bank of Canada for Canadians Coalition.   In a paper entitled "Reintegrating Monetary Policy Into the Economic Tool Kit" which he sent as an appendix to a February 4, 1994, letter to Gordon Thiessen, the new Governor of the Bank of Canada, one of Grant's proposals related to the $6 billion municipal infrastructure program which had been a key part of the platform of the new Liberal government elected in October, 1993. Grant's suggestion read as follows: "Given the severity of our current problems, we need to be pragmatic in looking for solutions. Under the existing legislation, the Bank of Canada can finance the entire $6-billion infrastructure program, provided the municipal debentures are guaranteed by either the federal or provincial levels. Let's do it as a first step. We can then assess its impact and determine whether or how far we should shift the balance of government borrowing and money creation from private lenders back towards the Bank of Canada. Increasing the proportion of effectively interest-free money and eliminating our reliance on foreign borrowing is the means to holding down the general level of interest rates. Such a shift is the key to reducing the government's single largest area of expenditure – interest on the public debt."[18]

THE SOVEREIGNTY PROPOSAL

A more comprehensive suggestion has been put forward in the United States by Kenneth Bohnsack. For several years he has been proposing that the United States Treasury be directed to create money and lend it, interest free, to junior tax supported bodies for voter-approved capital projects.   It is called the "Sovereignty Proposal".   Perhaps it isn't too surprising that the idea has been much more favorably received by the intended recipients than by those who would be charged with the implementation. I am advised that 1,828 tax supported bodies have endorsed the plan, as well as the U.S. Conference of Mayors representing 1,050 cities of 30,000 or more, where 80 million Americans reside; also the Bankers Association of Illinois, representing some 500 small banks, in addition to the House and Senate of Michigan.[19] Still the Sovereignty Proposal has many hurdles to overcome before the idea is accepted in mainstream economics.

In Canada a variant of the Bohnsack proposal was put forward by Jack Biddell in his 1993 book *A Self Reliant Future for Canada*. Biddell is one of Canada's best known and most respected accountants and trustees in bankruptcy. He has also had extensive experience in the administration of incomes policies and knows first-hand the consequences of the irrational monetary policy followed in recent years. His suggestion is the formation of two Bank of Canada funds bearing interest at 1 percent. Facility A would be a $100 billion debt refinancing fund which would allow the provincial governments to replace high interest debt with low as the existing debt matured. Facility B would be a $200 billion loan to the federal and provincial governments to be drawn on over the next 20 years. The B Facility would be divided into B1, a $175 billion pool for capital expenditures and/or industrial investment, and a B2 pool of $25 billion for deficit financing. The money for infrastructure would be repaid over the life of the bridge, tunnel or filtration plant being built.[20]

THE DEAD WEIGHT OF DOGMATISM

As I ponder the reasons why ideas which are so obviously beneficial to the public weal should be so deeply buried in the dust-covered book shelves of public libraries far from public consciousness, several come to mind. First, and most important, people don't understand the concept. And politicians, believe it or not, are people too and they don't understand it; so whenever they receive a submission on the subject they refer it to their congressional or parliamentary research staff for "expert" comment. The analyses are totally predictable. I have read a number of them and they are almost embarrassing in their "the sun does revolve 'round the earth and it's baloney to think otherwise" brand of dogmatism.

Occasionally there has been a politician who would understand and admit publicly to being intrigued by the potential. One man I remember was a long-ago mayor of Vancouver, Gerald (Gerry) DeGeer.[21] But his monetary views were considered an aberration and tolerated by a skeptical press only because he was so popular on every other front.

I often listened to the Social Credit MPs debate and was interested in what they had to say, but remained silent. I sometimes wondered if anyone else on the government benches felt the same way. You can imagine my astonishment when one day, as I was standing behind the curtain of the House of Commons, where we often stood when we were only half listening or when those who smoked wished to have a cigarette, one of my senior colleagues, David Croll, said "You know, what they are saying makes a lot of sense." I was flabbergasted. David Croll was on the left wing of the Liberal party and the Social Crediters were perceived as being on the far right. Croll had served his country in wartime, been mayor of Windsor, a cabinet minister in the provincial government of Ontario and resigned his portfolio during the dispute between the United Automobile Workers and General Motors of Canada when the union was trying to get a toe-hold. Croll's immortal line was "I would rather walk with the UAW than ride with General Motors." So anyone who knew him, and what he stood for, would have been as surprised as I was to hear him admit that a fundamental reform of the monetary system made sense.

I was perfectly aware, however, that if a reporter had stopped him on the way out of the House and asked him what he thought of the Social Credit speech just delivered he would have mumbled something like "nonsense" and dashed off. It would be hypocritical of me to suggest that I would have done otherwise. I don't know what I would have said but it certainly wouldn't have been complimentary. If either of us had been forthright we would have been labeled "nut cakes" or something equally unflattering.

To put it bluntly, we were intimidated by the press. I doubt that there were more than two or three of the several hundred reporters in the parliamentary press gallery who had the vaguest notion of how money was created and how the monetary system operated; and they were the ones who were not widely read. Syndicated columnists like Southam News' Charlie Lynch, for example, would just bellow "funny money" and go into hysterics anytime the subject was even alluded to. I hate to think what Charlie would have written about any allegedly "respected" member of one the major parties who uttered a sympathetic word.

For all his skill at writing Lynch was not particularly analytical. When I think of him I'm reminded of a chance meeting with Rabbi Abraham Feinberg of Toronto's Holy Blossom Synagogue at what is now Pearson International Airport. After exchanging a few pleasantries he said: "You politicians are just like us clergymen; too much time spent traveling and talking and not enough spent reading and thinking." I don't think it would be too unkind to put Charlie, who died a few weeks after this section was written, in the same boat with the politicians he wrote about. No doubt he was influenced by the many bank and securities firm economists who are routinely quoted by the media. It is assumed that they are neutral because they are economists but in fact they have a powerful vested interest in perpetuating the present system.

A second and related problem was that in Canada, at least, the Social Credit Party sometimes colored the objectivity of their case by alleging an international conspiracy of bankers. Conspiracy theories are never popular with mainstream politicians so that was reason enough for the majority to "tune out". Worse, there was occasionally just a whiff of anti-Semitism in the background. This was resented, and justly so. It was true that the Rothschilds had understood the advantages of fractional reserve banking and had used their knowledge skilfully to put some European governments deeply in their debt.[22] But the same can be said for Italian, French, Canadian, American, German and Japanese bankers. The cupidity of the bankers is less the result of a conspiracy on their part than a by-product of limited understanding on the part of governments and their electors.

A third obstacle has been the exaggerated claims of some monetary enthusiasts. A tabloid that arrived in my mail in July, 1994, proclaimed in respect of the Bank of Canada creation of debt-free money: "This will mean the end of debts, taxes, unemployment, bankruptcies, crises, wars!"[23] The claim is so ridiculous that it must be dismissed as fantasy. Regrettably the grain of truth was drowned in a sea of hyperbole.

Another impediment has been a confusion of specifics. My files contain at least a dozen proposals of which no two are the same. In Irving Fisher's *100% Money*, for example, he proposed the establishment of a "Currency Commission" which would buy bank assets for cash to the point where every commercial bank would have a cash reserve equal to 100% of its checking deposits - a state it would be required to maintain. As the banks would lose a large part of their interest-bearing assets they would be required to recover the lost income through service charges to their depositors.[24] Little wonder, then, that although Fisher managed to find two prominent bankers willing to support the idea the majority were strongly opposed.

Milton Friedman, well aware of the necessity to neutralize the bankers' objections, proposed paying interest on the 100% reserves. In *A Program For Monetary Stability* he said the following. "I shall depart from the original 'Chicago Plan of Banking Reform' in only one respect, though one that I think is of great importance. I shall urge that interest be paid on the 100% reserves. This step will both improve the economic results yielded by the 100% reserve system, and also, as a necessary consequence, render the system less subject to the difficulties of avoidance that were the bug-a-boo of the earlier proposals."[25] One of the serious problems, however, was what the rate of interest should be. "This problem of how to set the rate of interest is another issue that I feel most uncertain about and that requires more attention than I have given to it."[26] This is a concern I share and especially when I know how difficult it would be to ensure objectivity when banks are such generous supporters of the political system.

Of the other proposals I have mentioned each is limited in scope. Jordan Grant's recommendation was limited to pump priming to see how a revised system would work. Kenneth Bohnsack is proposing money creation for specific purposes in the realm of state and city infrastructure. Jack Biddell is proposing money for debt refinancing, infrastructure and deficit financing in Canada. In both the Bohnsack and Biddell proposals the funds would be earmarked for specific purposes and one wonders if that is necessarily the most efficient use of resources – especially if we are talking about long-term as opposed to short-term resolution of the monetary system.

In Chapter Seven, I will propose a variation on the theme which is intended to be general as opposed to specific in its application, and long-term as opposed to short-term in horizon. It is designed to stand the test of time, at least for a generation, after which such adjustments can be made as are deemed expedient on the basis of experience.

CONCLUSION

The concept of government-created debt-free money is time-honored and solid. Numerous conversations with the late Graham Towers, the first Governor of the Bank of Canada and one of the best financial minds Canada has produced, allayed any fears that I might have had on that score. He compared government-created money to Coca Cola and said "a bottle or two could be very refreshing whereas drinking a whole case at one sitting might kill you." These were wise words from a wise man who, throughout his career, always lived and upheld the maxim "moderation in all things."

CHAPTER 6

MAKE LOVE NOT WAR

"The century on which we are entering can be and must be the century of the common man."

Henry Wallace

      Before setting out recommended terms for the marriage contract between the two economies it may be useful to look at some of the aims and objects of public policy. What is it that you would like to accomplish? Is it full employment and maximum output? Or is it more important to maintain "hard" money for the benefit of those people who have cash to lend? Is it important to protect the external value of the dollar which is one by-product of low inflation and high interest rates? Or is it the smooth operation of the domestic economy which should rate top priority?

      Over the years I have developed my own set of priorities. In my own country I always deplored those times, including recent years since the U.S.-Canada Free Trade Agreement and then the North American Free Trade Agreement went into effect, when high interest rates were the bait to keep the Canadian dollar artificially over-valued at the expense of jobs at home. This masochistic policy reminded me of earlier

71

attempts to maintain a gold standard and the absurd consequence that ensued. I am firmly convinced that a smooth-running domestic economy should be the top priority of any national government and its monetary minions. It follows that the external value of a currency must be subordinate to that goal.

The next choice is between employment and inflation. If it were in fact a trade-off, as most economists stoutly affirm, I would be obliged to accept a little inflation - anything less than four or five percent – as a small price to pay for a high level of employment and output. It is true that inflation is a tax on the rich but if the purchasing power of their wealth can only be preserved by condemning hundreds of thousands of innocents to unemployment and poverty, the choice has to be made on moral grounds. A job equates with human dignity. The right to gainful employment is just as fundamental as freedom of speech and religion. In our complex societies a job is living expression of self-worth.

Fortunately the trade-off between employment and inflation is not as fundamental as we have been led to believe. It is largely a myth perpetrated by an inadequate analysis of the source of post-1950's inflation and consequently using the wrong medicine to control it. The much touted Phillips Curve, which allegedly predicts the trade-off, is a better reflection of economic history than an instrument of economic policy. In later chapters I will offer a personal prescription to control contemporary inflation as an alternative to the monetary roller-coaster that has literally taken our economic breath away. I will purport to show that it is possible to pursue the twin goals of full employment and stable prices simultaneously. For the purpose of this chapter, therefore, the emphasis will be exclusively on jobs.

Unquestionably one of the most disappointing and disillusioning consequences of the monetarist approach to inflation-fighting has been an unacceptably high level of unemployment. This has always bothered me and fresh salt was poured in the old wound early on the morning of May 19th, 1994, as I listened to a radio report of a question and answer period with Milton Friedman following his address at Vancouver's Fraser Institute the previous day. Question to Dr. Friedman:

"If you had been invited to the G-7 meeting on unemployment, what advice would you have provided to the ministers? Answer:

"I wouldn't have attended, ha, ha, but the answer is very simple. The problem that they were dealing with is unemployment, is a government-created problem, created by excessive regulation of the terms and conditions under which people can be employed. If you make it very expensive for people to employ people, they're going to employ fewer than if you don't, and what's happened in many of the western countries, including to a lesser extent the United States, is that the gap between the cost to the employer of hiring a person and the return to the employee from being hired, that gap has widened, and in some of the European countries it's 50%. If you take a place like France, where they have very high social security – so-called social security taxes – and the way to eliminate the unemployment is to open up the market, to free the markets, to let wages be determined by the market and to eliminate all of the extra costs that are piled on by extra regulation. It's hard to fire people. If it's hard to fire people, people will be very careful about hiring them, so I don't think that's a very complicated problem. What's complicated is the political [will]. Like so many of these [problems], it's easy to say what you should do, but it's very hard to do it, because of the political vested interests that are involved."[1]

As I listened intently I thought to myself: "This is a cop-out. This is the kind of answer politicians give to a question when they don't know the answer." I suspect that is the truth, and that monetarists really do not know how to square the human tragedy of involuntary idleness with the neat precision of their mathematical imperative.

Of course government regulations are an impediment to enterprise and certainly there are persons on Unemployment Insurance or welfare who are better off than they would be working at a minimum wage. But these conditions, which must be addressed if the system is ever to achieve its highest level of performance possible, do not come within a country mile of explaining the Organisation for Economic Co-operation and Development's projection of 35 million unemployed in 1995.[2] Ninety percent of the problem is the same one that has plagued western economies periodically for two hundred years, i.e. a shortage of aggregate demand, even if the reasons for it have changed.

How, then, can full employment – defined as a rough equilibrium between job seekers and job openings – be achieved? By declaring war? Curiously, I have never talked to anyone, even the most conservative of conservative economists, who doesn't agree that if the United States declared war tomorrow, and it turned out to be a protracted war, that full employment would be achieved within two years. One minute they are insisting that programs be cut and budgets balanced and a minute later, when cornered, they agree that in the event of war none of that would matter.

What would happen to make full employment possible? The federal government would start to recruit men and women for the armed forces and to let contracts for ships, planes, guns and ammunitions. Where would they get the money? No doubt there would be some increase in taxes but the bulk of the money would be either printed or borrowed and some of the money borrowed would almost certainly be new bank-created money. The government would run a big deficit. It would sell bonds to cover the deficit. Some of the bonds would be bought by the public from existing savings. Some would be bought by banks after the Fed provided the liquidity necessary to allow them to expand their lending capacity. Other bonds might be bought by individuals with the help of bank loans obtained for that purpose – loans that would only be possible thanks to the banks' licenses to expand the money supply. The net result of all this financial manoeuvring, however, would be a rapidly expanding economy and, soon, full employment.

Hasn't it ever struck you as peculiar that our best and brightest are quite capable of that kind of hat-trick in time of war, in order to produce a whole list of items that are of no earthly use except for killing, while they appear to be quite incapable of comparable ingenuity in winning the peace? It's time for another war, but not one of bombs and guns. It's time that we waged war against pollution, inadequate housing, illiteracy, sickness, poverty and hunger, decaying infrastructure, urban blight and, above all, indifference. Engaging in all these wars will be more than enough to achieve full employment; and it can be done without the inflation associated with a shooting war.

A WAR AGAINST POLLUTION

Few issues have risen from obscurity to first rank as quickly and dramatically as the preservation and protection of planet earth. The concept of sustainable growth which began with a few voices crying in the wilderness has become a global chorus of concern. Few documents have underlined the score as succinctly as the Report of the World Commission on Environment and Development headed by Norway's Prime Minister Gro Harlem Bruntland.[3] Her efforts, and those of her fellow commissioners, were a milestone in raising the consciousness of a complacent world. Had we translated that consciousness into action more quickly we might have prevented our North American fisheries from being depleted to the catastrophic extent they have been. The search for a sustainable future is more than just an abstract concept as both east and west coast fishermen have learned to their dismay.

The problem is a global one. In *Our World, Our Environment*, a U.S. Information Services publication, the foreword to an article entitled "Earth's Future Climate", by physicist James Trefil, sums up some of the ambivalence we face. "Early in 1991, the U.S. National Aeronautics and Space Administration and the British Meteorological Office reported that average temperatures on earth the year before had been the highest ever recorded. In fact, six of the seven warmest years on record occurred between 1981 and 1990. Many researchers interpret these data as evidence of a serious, continuing warming of the earth caused by pollutants in the atmosphere that trap heat close to the planet's surface - a phenomenon known as the greenhouse effect.   Other equally prominent scientists believe, however, that evidence of man-made global warming is inconclusive and that dire warnings of changes in the earth's environment are premature."[4]

Listening to the experts debate this issue reminds me of a decision I had to make a few years ago when I was bitten by a bat. I went to a doctor for advice. When I explained that there was no way to determine whether the bat was rabid or not he put my options this way.

"If the bat was not rabid you've no problem."

"And if it was", I asked?

"If it was, and you don't take the shots, you're dead.!" As I was never one inclined to play Russian Roulette in such matters I took the shots and lived to fight another day.

Similarly I do not think it is wise to gamble with our earthly habitat. It is far better to adopt the worse case scenario and continue the race to end the use of chlorofluorocarbons (CFC's) in a sprint to victory; to adopt effective plans to plant more trees than are uprooted or burned each year; to reduce air pollution and acid precipitation; to develop more energy-efficient refrigerators, cars and industrial plants. Dr. Trefil sums it up this way. "Deciding what to do about the greenhouse effect is like deciding how much insurance to buy. There is a risk, global warming. There is a costly solution, involving the eventual abandonment of fossil fuels. It seems to me that the proverbial prudent man should allocate some resources for insurance against the risk."[5]

Air and water know no boundaries and we are told that the next thirty years will be critical if we are going to restore the regenerative powers of our global habitat. The world's wealthier nations have begun their war to clean the air. In the United States much progress has been made. As Rob Brenner, Environmental Protection Agency acting deputy assistant administrator for air and radiation, said at a news briefing November 2, 1993. "Over the 10 years ending in 1992, improvements were 89 percent for lead, 34 percent for carbon monoxide, 23 percent for sulfur dioxide, 21 percent for ozone,

17 percent for particles of soot and 8 percent for nitrogen dioxide", six of the most harmful of the widely found contaminants.[6] "This is not the time to relax", added Brenner. "About 53.6 million persons in 1992 lived in areas that do not meet the health standards for at least one of the pollutants."[7]

Worldwide, the war has just begun. The United States and the former Soviet Union are still the largest emitters of sulfur oxides, but an increase in these pollutants is seen in China, Mexico and India. Estimates of global particulate matter emissions vary from 57 to 135 million tons a year. Cleaner-burning technology has led to decreased emissions in industrialized countries. Eastern Europe and developing countries that lack this technology have seen increases in the pollutant.

The search for purer water is another area of concern. In the February 11, 1994 issue of the *CQ Researcher* an article entitled "Water Quality", by Richard L. Worsnop, cites the challenge. "In March and April, nearly 400,000 people in the Milwaukee area became ill – and six died – from an intestinal parasite that invaded the municipal water supply. Similar but less serious water problems occurred later in the year in New York City and Washington, D.C. That wasn't all. Severe flooding of the Mississippi River and its major tributaries disabled the water-treatment systems in Des Moines, Iowa, and hundreds of other Midwestern communities.

"To experts who say the nation's drinking water is not nearly as safe as it should be, the events of 1993 were only a grim warning of what could lie ahead. U.S. tap water is teeming with contaminants, these critics charge, adding that new harmful substances are joining the list virtually every day. The more worrisome contaminants include disease-causing micro-organisms, lead, nitrates, arsenic and radon. Even chlorine, the most widely used disinfectant in U.S. water-treatment systems, is now viewed as a potential hazard."[8]

The challenge of purifying air and water applies equally on both sides of the Canada - U.S. border. Polluted air and acid rain are not subject to customs inspection in either direction. We also share the Great Lakes basin which contains nearly 20 percent of the world's fresh water and 95 percent of the fresh water of the United States. As Carol M. Browner, administrator, United States Environmental Protection Agency pointed out on March 31, 1993, in announcing an innovative ecosystem approach to protecting the basin: "The Lakes and their tributaries provide a source of drinking water for over 23 million people. They also are home to 25 percent of U.S. industry. The Lakes serve as habitat to hundreds of species of mammals, birds, reptiles, amphibians, fish, and plant life. They provide recreation and beauty for millions of Americans.

"Toxic pollutants in the Lakes originate from a multitude of sources, including municipal and industrial discharges, wet weather runoff, and atmospheric deposition. These pollutants place this great natural resource and the residents of the region at risk. States have identified toxic substances as the most extensive cause of water quality damages in the Great Lakes basin. The Great Lakes are extremely vulnerable to persistent pollutants that accumulate in the tissues of fish and wildlife. As a result, the ecosystem's wildlife have reproductive defects and tumors. Human health is threatened through consumption of fish and shellfish."[9] It goes without saying that cleaning up the basin has to be a cooperative effort between Canada and the U.S. and that the cost to each country will be many billions of dollars.

Without shirking our share of responsibility worldwide we have to begin by cleaning up our own backyard. Canadians lead the world in garbage generated per person[10] and Americans are running hard to overtake us. *The Garbage Primer* tells the U.S. story. "The amount of garbage we throw out in this country has more than doubled over the past 30 years, while the population has increased by only 38 percent. In 1960, Americans threw out 88 million tons of garbage and by 1990 we were filling our trash cans with 195.7 million tons of waste. If we do not change our ways, we will usher in the 21st century with more than 222 million tons of garbage a year. The greatest increases are in nondurable items such as paper and clothing, durable items such as appliances and tires, and containers and packaging."[11] (See Figure 5)

After the Trash Can

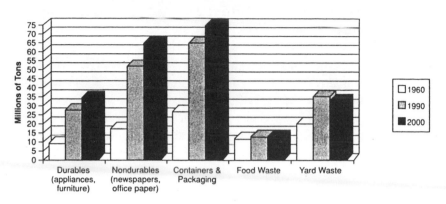

Figure 5

Types of products generated in the waste stream 1960 to 2000, in millions of tons. This graph represents generation before materials recovery or combustion; it does not include construction and demolition debris or industrial process wastes. Source: Adapted from EPA, Characterization of Municipal Solid Waste in the United States: 1992 Update.

"Underlying this current debate on solid waste management is the more fundamental debate of how we should pay for waste management. Some hold the consumer ultimately responsible and believe that, as taxpayers, we should pay the local government to dispose of the waste we create. Others believe that industry should be held responsible for the waste it generates, and that waste management costs should be built into product costs and paid by the product producers and consumers."[12] In the long run it really doesn't matter too much which pocket the cash comes from and the issue is unlikely to be resolved in terms of black and white. The important thing is to get the job done and innovation is breaking out all over.

Consumer attitudes are changing and with it a review of business practices. In an article entitled, "The U.S. Disposes of the Way it Disposes – By Recycling", Kevin Pearce cites a number of positive developments. "With consumer awareness on the rise, a number of forward-thinking corporations have adopted waste-reduction measures. The McDonald's restaurant chain, for example, earned kudos for working with the Environmental Defence Fund to develop an ambitious reduction and recycling program that could cut down its paper and plastic waste by millions of pounds per year."[13]

Some cities have led the way. "Seattle beat its trash problem with an innovative program that reduces waste and saves money. Now the rest of the country is following suit."[14] Much progress has been made for which we are all thankful. But without minimizing what has been done the point has to be made that the war has just begun and that it will be around for a long time.

A WAR AGAINST INADEQUATE HOUSING

I might have titled this a war against homelessness except the problem is much broader than that and there is a wave of resentment building against America's most dis-enfranchised people. In an article in *Time* magazine in December, 1993, Jill Smolowe put changing public attitudes in perspective. "The sympathy of the 1980's that gave way to compassion fatigue by the turn of the decade is now an open expression of loathing for the homeless. Once romanticized as impoverished casualties of an uncaring society, America's homeless – who number anywhere from 600,000 to 3 million, depending on whose count you believe – are now more likely to be demonized as pathological predators who spoil neighborhoods and threaten the commonweal."[15]

In a November 1993 column in *U.S. News and World Report*, John Leo wrote: "A consensus of researchers says 40 percent of homeless adults are alcoholics. One study puts the figure at 66 percent. A 1992 New York study found that 83 percent of single adults in homeless shelters tested positive for cocaine. Nationally, up to 85 percent of all homeless are alcoholics, drug addicts or mentally ill."[16]

Street-smart liberal columnist Pete Hamill asserts that homelessness is a public-health problem spawned by "drunks, crackheads or crazies." Jill Smolowe's *Time* article went on to say: "Calling for 'tough-love' solutions, Hamill offers a

startling proposal: quarantine male street people on military
bases and compel them to accept medical treatment. 'The men
would be treated as menaces to the public health, not as
criminals,' [Hamill] writes. Yet under this prescription those
who resist such attentions 'would be charged with crimes of
violence and turned over to the criminal-justice system.'"[17]

While this extreme proposal does not attract official
interest, Smolowe cites a more gentle approach that appears
promising. "In Orlando, Florida, the 30,000-sq.-ft. Coalition
Campus offers one-stop-shopping for the area's homeless.
Unlike most cities' shelters, which typically screen out people
who are drunk or drugged, the Orlando facility provides beds
for as many as 700 people, no matter how sorry their state.
The facility, which is open around the clock, offers substance
abuse and mental-health counselling, plus adult education
courses and such basic amenities as telephones and mail service.
All this is free, and people can stay as long as they want. Since
opening last September, the $1.3 million-a-year facility, funded
by government and private money has produced immediate
benefits for the community. 'Petty crime has dropped about
40% to 50% downtown,' says Michael Poole, head of the
Coalition for the Homeless of Central Florida. 'There's cost
savings in police time and prison beds.' Dade County
commissioners are so impressed that they aim to open three
similar facilities with grant money and funds collected from the
1 cents tax they recently levied on large restaurants."[18]

It appears not only desirable, but essential that
something be done. Apart from the fact that street people are
human beings and consequently deserving of some concern,
when their presence fills a neighborhood with fear and appre-
hension there is a self-serving motive at least as powerful as the
altruistic one. Health care and housing are both hand-maidens
of reform.

The question of inadequate housing extends far beyond
immediate shelter for street people, of course. It covers the
habitation of tens of thousands of people who are neither sick
nor mentally handicapped. They are the poor who can't bridge
the gap between income and rent. Either an increase in income

or decent housing at more affordable rates would help ends to meet.

The Fed's 1994 interest rate policy has made the situation worse instead of better. In the August 17, 1994 *Wall Street Journal*, David Lehreah, chief economist of the Mortgage Bankers Association, predicted that rates on 3-year mortgages will rise to about 9% by year end. "They were at 7.2% in February, before the Fed's first move to boost short-term rates. The steady climb already has frozen 200,000 home buyers out of the market, he estimates. 'Now we're probably talking another 50,000 added to that,' he said."[19]

A WAR AGAINST ILLITERACY

A September 1993 press release from the United States Department of Education is titled "Literacy Levels Deficient for 90 Million U.S. Adults". It reads, in part: "Some 90 million adults – about 47 percent of the U.S. adult population – demonstrate low levels of literacy, according to a nationwide study released today by the U.S. Department of Education. However, according to *Adult Literacy in America*, most of these adults describe themselves as being able to read or write English 'well' or 'very well'.

"'This report is a wake-up call to the sheer magnitude of illiteracy in this country and underscores literacy's strong connection to economic status,' U.S. Secretary of Education Richard W. Wiley said. 'It paints a picture of a society in which the vast majority of Americans do not know that they do not have the skills they need to earn a living in our increasingly technological society and international marketplace.'

"'Even though many people do not perceive themselves as 'at risk,' the findings show that adults with lower literacy skills are far less likely to work full-time, to earn high wages, or to vote,' the Secretary added. 'Since those with low literacy skills are far more likely to live in poverty, we must work to ensure that those adults who are just 'getting by' today will not be left behind by progress in a global economy, by the rapid advances in technology, and by the transformation of the work-place. As President Clinton has said, we do not have a person to waste.' "[20]

The Canadian situation is just as worrisome.   The Canadian Business Task Force on Literacy estimated that one million Canadians can neither read nor write. These are the hard core cases but there are approximately 5 million adults with reading skills below the grade 9 level. While enhanced education is not a guarantee of employment and while many college graduates require additional training in order to qualify for specific jobs, and education by itself does not guarantee high income, the data for both countries show that there is a correlation between education and earning power. This has always been true but will be even more so in future. As Alan Eck reminds us in the *Monthly Labor Review*: "Large numbers of high-paying production jobs that required unskilled workers to repeat simple tasks have been greatly reduced. The work-place has been reorganized, and more jobs now require reading, mathematics, and communication skills."[21]

One area in which literacy training produces above average dividends is with prison inmates. Their mastery of the three R's is often well below the standard required for successful job-seekers. So they face a double handicap as they leave prison and seek work - the stigma of a prison record in addition to inadequate schooling. Teaching prisoners to read and write, as well as some trade in reasonable demand in the market place, will inevitably enhance their opportunities and reduce the recidivism rate.

A WAR AGAINST SICKNESS

Few subjects are more controversial than how health care should be administered. Few fears are greater than the fear of serious illness for someone without insurance who faces the prospect of financial ruin in the wake of a tidal wave of medical bills. Few businesses involve as much money and as many deeply entrenched financial interests as the business of providing health care. Consequently, while there is near universal agreement that something must be done to make the system fairer and more universally accessible, there is little consensus about the best way to achieve that goal.

At the time our Canadian system was being discussed, my cabinet colleagues were deeply concerned about the need for universal access, but most simply heaved a sigh of resignation when it came to questions of bureaucratic excess and possible abuse. They considered all the positive aspects of the Swedish and British models but turned a blind eye to the defects which were becoming more in evidence as the systems matured.

I proposed an alternative scheme of universal insurance under which everyone would pay their own medical bills up to 2% of their gross income and be 100% insured for the balance. The advantages included access to the best medical care for rich and poor alike; minimum red-tape; and the least incentive for people who can well afford their own routine "throat checks" to take advantage of the system and demand services just because they are "free". During the discussion every minister, without exception, said it was a better system. Unfortunately, however, a heavy-weight who had the ear of the prime minister, and who was the last to speak, added: "But it wouldn't be politic."[22] That was the end of the discussion. All rational debate had ended.

The system we adopted served us well for two decades and is still infinitely better than U.S. newspaper reports about it that read as if they were written from another planet. Now, however, the system is in trouble as a direct result of the two monetarist recessions. The resulting increases in government deficits, federal and provincial, have meant cutbacks in funding to the point where fewer people are entitled to fewer services, hospital beds are being taken out of service, care-givers are overworked, and queues for many critical procedures are extending. Only a massive monetary infusion or radical surgery can restore the system. In addition to the choice as to what system can best serve all citizens, and acceptance of the fact that anything that is satisfactory in principle will cost vast sums for individuals, business or governments, there will be an ongoing war to develop better medicines, improve techniques and make knowledge and technology available to the world's sick. It is a war worthy of our finest strategists and technicians.

A WAR AGAINST DECAY

It has been estimated that both the U.S. and Canada will have to spend tens of billions of dollars replacing our urban infrastructure: roads, bridges, sewers, and watermains in the next decade or two just to keep from getting swamped with the breakdowns. Robert B. Reich put the magnitude of the task in perspective in *The Work of Nations: Preparing Ourselves for 21st Century Capitalism*: "In the 1950's, the nation committed itself to building a modern transportation system. Infrastructure then absorbed over 6 percent of the nation's non-military budget each year, or just under 4 percent of gross national product, where it remained through most of the 1960's. Public spending on the nation's transportation system declined in the 1970's, and declined even more sharply in the 1980's, to the point where the nation was spending only 1.2 percent of its non-military budget on building and maintaining infrastructure. Hence the specter of collapsing bridges and crumbling highways. In 1989, the U.S. Department of Transportation estimated that simply to repair the nation's 240,000 bridges would require an expenditure of $50 billion; to repair the nation's highways, $315 billion. Spending on new infrastructure has fallen even more dramatically, from 2.3 percent of GNP in 1963 to only 1 percent in 1989."[23]

Everyone knows that at some point in the life of infrastructure the time comes when it is more expensive to maintain than to replace. The situation in the United States is the same as the one in Canada where we have reached that stage with many of our installations and if we don't act soon the backlog will be incredible. It is another case of an ounce of prevention being better than a pound of cure. A planned program, starting now, will enable us to cope; and at a manageable cost. A long range program will make most efficient use of the expertise and equipment required by amortizing both over many years. If we don't act now the opposite will be true. We will need a crash program with its inevitable mistakes and unreasonably high costs.

Studies have shown that the efficiency of any economic machine is influenced by the quality of its infrastructure. It is just one more area where our two countries can continue to fall behind or catch up and improve our competitiveness.

A WAR AGAINST URBAN BLIGHT

One of the most vivid impressions I gained as chairman of Canada's 1969 Task Force on Housing and Urban Development was the contrast between the best and the worst within our cities. The best was excitingly beautiful – a kind of urban fairyland. The worst was movingly described in our report. "Here, too, is poverty in its rawest and ugliest form. No pretty gardens or painted cottages here to camouflage economic depression. Poverty in the worst areas of the city core is abundantly visible in the decrepit structures which form its housing, the cracked pavement of the streets which are its recreational area, and the rodents which are its wild life. This poverty you can see – and hear – and taste – and smell. Its residents are not simply families struggling to catch up to the average national income; too often they are people fighting to retain a vestige of human dignity and self-respect. No Task Force impression is more vivid of mind or depressing of spirit than those formed amid the blight and slum of Canada's larger cities."[24]

As someone who has visited many of America's largest cities, I hope it will not be considered presumptuous to say that the problem in the U.S. is every bit as real, and perhaps more so. To cite another outside opinion, an editorial in the *Economist*, there is much reason for concern, but also hope. "Walk, if you dare, through the worst parts of urban America – New York's Bronx, Chicago's South Side, East St. Louis, South-Central Los Angeles. The burned-out blocks, the boarded-up businesses, the ubiquitous hoodlums and gang warfare, suggest that these places should simply be abandoned. Cities, like the people who live in them, have a natural cycle. Yet the decline of America's inner cities is far from irreversible. Much of what is wrong with these places can be traced to plain bad government. That can be changed."[25]

I do not believe that the problems of the inner cities can be solved by just throwing more money at them. As the *Economist* points out: "Today, 65 cents of every dollar of federal aid for the urban poor is absorbed by the urban bureaucracy that is supposed to deliver it."[26] So money alone won't do the trick. As Thomas Sowell puts it in commenting on Professor Edward C. Banfield's book, *The Unheavenly City*, what is required is "not just a re-examination of particular fallacies but a re-examination of the whole framework of misconceptions behind the urban disasters of our times."[27]

Taming entrenched bureaucracies will provide one of the major battles. Both jobs and loss of face are at stake. Re-examining the distribution of taxes is another. As Warren Cohen reported in *U.S. News & World Report* in an article entitled "Cities try to bring home the bacon; job creation is still a struggle for urban America."

"Cities face two major disadvantages in attracting jobs today. First, there is pitched competition from states, which tend to lure companies to locations in suburban, ex-urban or even rural areas. Alabama landed a new factory from German auto maker Mercedes-Benz in exchange for tax breaks, job-training money and infrastructure improvements – incentives that amount to an estimated $169,000 per job. Cash-strapped cities can't match these giveaways because of severe fiscal difficulties. Since 1980, federal aid to cities has been sliced in half, from $47 billion to $24 billion. This decline and an urban exodus have increased the tax burden on those who remain in the cities. In 1980, cities derived 63 percent of their revenues from local sources; by 1991, that figure had grown to 72 percent. Crime is the second problem cities have in attracting companies. The crime rate in the 25 largest U.S. cities in 1992 was 60 percent higher than the national average, a figure that helps explain why businesses are leaving them."[28]

There is no easy answer to these problems. Some liberals blame all the ills on society. Not so, says Professor Banfield. The crucial variable in urban riots, or in much of the other urban pathology, is not a matter of race, but a matter of cultural values and reckless behavior – "an outlook and style of life which is radically present-oriented, and which therefore attaches no value to work, sacrifice, self-improvement, or service to family, friends, or community."[29]

At the risk of being a fence-sitter I believe there is much truth on both sides. Some citizens have been denied "equal opportunity". At the same time blaming someone else is no solution and the concept of individual responsibility has to be re-popularized. In the newspapers I read, the word "rights" appears fifty times as often as the word "responsibility". Of one thing I am certain. Although the war will be difficult, frustrating and long-term it can be won – and it is worth the fight.

My own city of Toronto is a pretty good example of one that has successfully revitalized the city core. It is now interesting, a good place to visit, a preferred place to live and about as safe as any city of its size anywhere.

SUMMARY

The purpose of this chapter is to demonstrate that there is no shortage of work to be done in the public and private sectors. A combination of citizens needs and wants – which are different for rich and poor – are sufficient to provide everyone with useful employment for many years to come. If the needs and wants can't be translated into jobs, that is the fault of the system which, because it hasn't been intelligently operated for some time, has created a number of "solutions" that don't make any sense – except in the unreal environment of the moment. These include job sharing where I am in complete accord with the opinion expressed in the OECD Jobs Study under the heading "What the Answer is Not." "Legislated, across-the-board work-sharing addresses the unemployment problem not by increasing the number of jobs through more economic activity, but through rationing gainful work."[30] The same objection applies to mandatory early retirement to provide openings for the young, a demand for a shorter work week as another form of job sharing and acceptance of an "unnatural" rate of unemployment which is accepted as natural by people who don't understand the cause of stagflation.

My belief is that citizens should be given the widest range of choice possible. If they prefer more leisure as an alternative to higher income, okay. If for reasons of personal preference or convenience two people want to share work, that is fine as long as labor unit costs don't rise as a result. If people want to work past normal retirement age, and there is no question of public safety involved, that option should be available to them. Above all, people who want to work as a means of satisfying their needs and aspirations should be able to find work within a reasonable period. All of these choices would be within the realm of the possible if the system were changed significantly as recommended in subsequent chapters.

CHAPTER 7

A 50% SOLUTION

*"Throw no gyft agayne at the gevers head for better is halfe
a lofe than no bread."*

John Haywood

Monetary reform alone will not solve all economic problems. Other measures, including an incomes policy and tighter banking regulations to be discussed in subsequent chapters, are required. A revolutionary change in the way money is created, however, is the bedrock foundation on which a more stable and enduring system can be built. Without monetary reform the whole economic superstructure will sink deeper and deeper into debt.

Bank "admirers" with a penchant for vengeance might fantasize a solution along the lines of the one adopted by England's King Charles II. He just repudiated liability for the deposits held in the Exchequer.

"This King being always in want of money, and not wishing to go before the House of Commons, took counsel of his ministers as to the best way of obtaining money without the aid of Parliament. The King promised a reward of the Lord Treasurer's post to whoever would suggest the means. The idea of closing the Exchequer occurred to Lord Ashley, who unguardedly communicated it to Sir Thomas Clifford, and he immediately unfolded the plan before the King, who was charmed at the idea of such perfidy, and exclaimed: 'Odds fish! I will be as good as my word if you can find me the money.' Accordingly the Exchequer was closed on the 2nd of January 1672, and all payments to the goldsmith-bankers suspended; this not only brought ruin to them, but to many thousands of their customers.   Sir Thomas Clifford was made Lord High Treasurer and a peer."[1]

It was only intended as a temporary measure and some interest was subsequently paid; but the goldsmiths never did get their money back.[2] It was an extreme solution and not really appropriate to Charles' time or ours.

Somewhat less extreme was Yale economist Irving Fisher's suggestion that the banks be required to exchange their interest-bearing assets for cash (to be provided by a 'Currency Commission' on behalf of the government) up to an amount equal to 100% of their checking deposits.[3] It is still interesting, decades later when the Great Depression is only a distant memory, to read the list of advantages Fisher said would accrue to the public. They are as follows:

"1. There would be practically no more runs on commercial banks; because 100% of the depositors' money would always be in the bank (or available) awaiting their orders. In practice, less money would be withdrawn than now; we all know of the frightened depositor who shouted to the bank teller 'If you haven't got my money, I want it; if you have, I don't.'

2. There would be far fewer bank failures; because the important creditors of a commercial bank who would be most likely to make it fail are its depositors, and these depositors would be 100% provided for.

3. The interest bearing Government debt would be substantially reduced; because a great part of the outstanding bonds of the Government would be acquired from the banks by the Currency Commission (representing the Government).

4. Our Monetary System would be simplified; because there would be no longer any essential difference between pocket-book money and check-book money. All of our circula-

ting medium, one hundred per cent of it, would be actual money.

5. Banking would be simplified; at present, there is a confusion of ownership. When money is deposited in a checking account, the depositor still thinks of that money as his, though legally it is the bank's. The depositor owns no deposit; he is merely a creditor of a private corporation. Most of the 'mystery' of banking would disappear as soon as a bank was no longer allowed to lend out money deposited by its customers, while, at the same time, these depositors were using that money as *their* money by drawing checks against it.

'Mr. Dooley,' the Will Rogers of his day, brought out the absurdity of this double use of money on demand deposit when he called a banker 'a man who takes care of your money by lending it out to his friends.'"[4]

While there is little doubt that the public would reap the advantages cited by Fisher the banks would be devastated by such a precipitous loss of income. Many banks already charge for the services such as cashing checks for example, that Fisher mentioned as an alternative source of revenue. In retrospect it is little wonder that bankers were less than enthusiastic about his proposal. To go from a position of low liquidity and high earnings to one of high liquidity and low earnings was not their view of bankers' heaven.

Milton Friedman implicitly acknowledged the reality of the situation when he suggested paying the banks interest on their converted assets. This way the loss of revenue would be vastly reduced and they would, theoretically at least, be able to cope quite nicely. Certainly it would avoid the massive instability that would attach to either the Fisher or King Charles II solutions, and that is important at a time when we desperately need greater stability rather than less. It would be the people, through their government, who would pay the banks interest on their cash reserves, however, so the benefit to taxpayers would be dubious at best.

Although Friedman has not renounced his support for a 100% reserve system it is no longer on his priority list as indicated in a footnote reply to a 1983 letter from William F.

Hixson. "As good a reform as ever," Friedman wrote, "...
unfortunately with as little prospect of adoption as ever. I keep
mentioning it but feel that tilting at windmills is not an effective
way to spend my time."[5] If he had been content to let it go at
that, the Nobel laureate would have earned a place among the
forward-looking thinkers on a fundamentally important issue.
But in subsequent writings he has recommended freezing the
production of government money and the adoption of zero
percent reserves.

In a 1986 letter to Professor John H. Hotson, in reply
to one on the subject of reserves and government-created
money, he wrote: "In my opinion, either extreme is acceptable.
I have not given up advocacy of one-hundred percent reserves.
I would prefer one-hundred percent reserves to the alternative
I set forth. However, I believe that getting the government out
of the business altogether or zero percent reserves also makes
sense. The virtue of either one is that it eliminates government
meddling in the lending and investing activities of the financial
markets. When I wrote in 1948, we were already halfway
toward one-hundred percent reserves because so large a fraction
of the assets of the banks consisted of either government bonds
or high-powered money. One-hundred percent reserves at that
time did not look impossible of achievement. We have moved
so far since then that I am very skeptical indeed that there is
any political possibility of achieving one-hundred percent
reserves. That does not mean that it is not desirable."[6]

Professor Friedman goes on to say that the sole reason
he stressed the zero percent reserves was "because it seemed
to me at least to be within the imaginable range of political
feasibility."[7] He was correct on that point as three countries,
including Canada, have already done it. But that doesn't mean
it makes sense. One could argue that it is one of the worst
ideas to emerge from the academy in the history of economics.
What Friedman is suggesting is a system based almost exclusively on debt which is the inverted pyramid that Irving
Fisher found so worrisome. It is the same inverted pyramid,
grotesquely exaggerated in recent decades, which makes the
present system inherently unstable. One has to be skeptical of

a theory based on political expediency rather than common sense.

It is my opinion that, as of now, neither extreme is acceptable. A zero reserve system, with its incredible leverage, is not only inherently unstable it will ultimately implode with a world-shattering crash. A 100% reserve system is not really feasible either due to the size and importance of the banking industry and its need to have some revenues in addition to the growing list of service charges. So it seems that a pragmatic, middle of the road course should be the order of the day – a solution that will reduce leverage to a sound level, contain the rise in the ratio of debt to GDP and still keep the banks in business.

No matter what one thinks about the banks as an industry they do perform some useful and essential functions. They are convenient places to park your money until you need it – assuming, of course, that you can get it back when you want it. The checking facilities they provide are absolutely essential to the smooth functioning of a highly-sophisticated economic system. They also play a role in the allocation of resources. They have done this abominably in recent years but bankers have the training and capacity to do it reasonably well if they were subject to explicit guidelines. Banks are already in place, so it would be far better to establish "rules of conduct" to ensure that money lent is consistent with the public interest than to establish competing government facilities that would be no more efficient in performing the function and, probably, much less efficient.

On the assumption, then, that a widely decentralized banking system can play an integral part in a stable system, it is both permissible and desirable to leave them with their existing interest-bearing paper as a source of revenue. It is also expedient to renew or extend their licenses to "print" money (create deposits) but only to the extent that is consistent with the public interest - which should be about half of the proportion of new money that they have become accustomed to creating.

It would be difficult to argue that the U.S. is in need

of much economic stimulus in 1994/95 in the face of the Fed deliberately putting on the brakes. Capacity utilization in manufacturing has been creeping up – enough that expansion plans are in the works. Unemployment remains well above historic lows, however, and the economy as a whole is still operating at a level below its potential.

So I have had econometric simulations run for two cases to illustrate what is possible. The first involves only the adoption of an incomes policy along the lines of the one recommended in Chapter 10. The results show that it, alone, would achieve full employment – about 4% unemployed – in 4 years, and with substantially less inflation than presently forecast. The second case includes a modest $15 billion a year stimulation directed at a few target areas such as upgrading the existing housing stock and the rehabilitation of urban cores. This would provide employment for low and semi-skilled workers and increase real output without generating any significant inflationary pressures. In addition the second case includes the infusion of significant amounts of government-created money each year until the banks' liabilities to reserves ratio falls to some reasonable level after which the banks and the government would split the money creation function 50% each.

Opponents of government-created money insist that the policy would be inflationary. They base their case on the pretence, and it is pretence, that the reserve requirements of the banking system would remain unchanged and that the infusion of such a vast amount of high-powered money (cash) would produce an explosion in the money supply (credit) followed by inflation rampant. This is nonsense! The reserve requirements of the banks would be consistently raised to the point where the total increase in the money stock – government-created money plus bank-created money – would be exactly the same as would have been the case otherwise. So the inflationary effects, if any, would not be altered. The only difference would be that the government would be printing more money and the banks would be "printing" less.

The institutional framework is important. There is, in theory at least, no reason why the Federal Reserve System couldn't be the custodian and operator of the new system provided its jurisdiction was extended to all banks as it is essential that all deposit-taking institutions be subject to the same reserve requirements. It has the advantage of being in existence and having offices (Federal Reserve Banks) in all geographical regions. An off-setting disadvantage would be the necessity of replacing most, if not all, of the Governors and senior staff. Their attitudes and utterances have been so pro-bank that they would appear to be psychologically incapable of adapting to a reformed system. Another disadvantage is that the Federal Reserve System is an expensive system!

An alternative would be to create a new Bank of the United States wholly owned by the people and staffed by committed reformers. A re-incarnated BUS would have the advantage of starting with a clean slate unencumbered by the Fed's dismal record beginning almost from the time it was created. But that is a decision that only the Congress in its wisdom can make. The most important criterion is clear lines of authority and a regulatory framework that will permit fast and sensitive action.

At the beginning of each year the central bank would set up a credit in the name of the U.S. Treasury in an amount of never more than 100 percent, and never less than 50 percent, of the real increase in output of the economy for the previous year, adjusted for the velocity of circulation of money and any significant change in demographics or anticipated participation rates. The Treasury could issue checks against this account at the rate of one-twelfth – seasonally adjusted to accommodate the rhythm of fiscal expenditures and receipts – each month. It would then spend the money into circulation as part of its ordinary expenditures. To prevent excessive (inflationary) multiple creation of money on the basis of the newly-created cash money, it would probably be necessary for the central bank to raise the private banks' reserve requirements monthly in the early stages but it would have to have sufficient leeway to compensate for any unexpected changes in the velocity of circulation and other unpredictables.

In view of the long-established penchant of central

bankers to maintain balanced books, the Treasury would sell the central bank common shares in the U.S. with a par value of some arbitrary amount – say $10 billion a share – which the central bank would keep on its books at cost as an asset against the "liability" of the credit or currency issued. This is preferable to the pledge of non-interest-bearing bonds which would perpetuate the upward trend of debt to GDP rather than bend the curve in the other direction.

Although the central bank should have day-to-day autonomy it should never, for obvious reasons, have absolute autonomy. Much blood was shed in getting rid of autocratic kings and our hard-won democracy, though "the worst of all possible systems", as Winston Churchill said, is still "better than all others", as he quickly added. So when it comes to monetary policy the best system would be one where the Secretary of the Treasury, as the people's representative, would be the final arbiter. The safeguard should be that any directives to the central bank (or Fed) would have to be in writing and would have to be made public so voters would have the information necessary to decide whether or not their interests were being well served.

As an enforcement measure, the deductibility of interest, for tax purposes, could only be allowed when the loan came from an institution maintaining the reserve levels required by the U.S. central bank. That would maintain a level playing field with foreign banks making loans in U.S. dollars. If anyone were clever enough to circumvent these regulations by using non-bank third parties, for example, the interest would not only be non-deductible, but subject to a penalty tax as well.

Someone, either the central bank or the Treasury, should also have standby power over margin requirements for all kinds of credit. I will return to the subject of margins later, but here I am thinking about the power to increase minimum monthly payments on credit card balances in the event that consumer purchases began to overheat the economy; and to require higher equity to debt ratios for either residential or non-residential real estate, or both, in case the construction industry started to bid up prices. Non-residential construction is one of the few exceptional cases where there has been demand inflation in the few cities where the banking system went berserk with its lending practices. This is a perfect example of where the brakes could have been applied in one industry, in relevant locations, without the necessity of carpet-bombing the whole economy.

Subject to these considerations, and the imposition of guidelines to limit the abuse of monopoly power which will be discussed in later chapters, it should be possible and certainly much easier to (a) balance government budgets, (b) reduce interest rates and allow the economy to grow at a faster rate while reducing debt service charges for governments and industry alike, (c) maintain price stability, i.e. annual increases in the Consumer Price Index in the order of 1 percent or less, (d) achieve a higher level of employment and (e) end the current increase in debt to GDP ratios.

ECONOMETRIC SIMULATIONS

The econometric simulations begin with a "base" or "reference" case which represents the consensus of a number of well-known economists as to how the economy is likely to perform. When new assumptions are added the model measures the impact as a variation from the base case.

U.S. CASE #1

Assumptions:
The implementation of an incomes policy to limit the excesses of monopoly power as set out in Chapter 10. In this case the effect on gross domestic product is very slight, ranging from a $5 billion decrease in year one to a $59 billion increase in year seven representing almost a 1% gain. On the employment side, however the gain is very significant bringing the level down to 4% in five years without any additional stimulation.[8]

YR.	1995	1996	1997	1998	1999	2000	2001

Comparison of New Policy with base case:

Unemployment Rate:

	1995	1996	1997	1998	1999	2000	2001
Base	6.20	5.90	5.63	5.52	5.46	5.46	5.47
New	6.12	5.57	4.95	4.41	4.00	3.79	3.68

Consumer Price Index: (1987 = 100)

	1995	1996	1997	1998	1999	2000	2001
Base	152.90	157.12	161.45	165.83	170.30	174.76	179.28
New	151.42	152.34	153.61	155.06	156.22	157.31	158.40

Bank Prime Rate:

	1995	1996	1997	1998	1999	2000	2001
Base	6.22	6.46	6.50	6.50	6.50	6.50	6.54
New	6.07	5.88	5.69	5.59	5.46	5.30	5.20

U.S. CASE #2

Assumptions:

A $15 billion stimulation for the rehabilitation of housing and city cores identified as STIM, the infusion of government-created money as GCM, plus the incomes policy as in Case #1.

YR.	1995	1996	1997	1998	1999	2000	2001
STIM $b.	15	15	15	15	15	15	15
GCM $b.	175	150	125	100	75	60	60

Plus the Incomes Policy as in Case #1.

Comparison of New Policy with base case:

Unemployment Rate:

	1995	1996	1997	1998	1999	2000	2001
Base	6.20	5.90	5.63	5.52	5.46	5.46	5.47
New	6.03	5.32	4.80	4.51	4.29	4.15	4.03

Consumer Price Index: (1987 = 100)

	1995	1996	1997	1998	1999	2000	2001
Base	152.90	157.12	161.45	165.83	170.30	174.76	179.28
New	151.51	152.49	153.81	155.32	156.56	157.74	158.94

Prime Rate:

	1995	1996	1997	1998	1999	2000	2001
Base	6.22	6.46	6.50	6.50	6.50	6.50	6.54
New	5.91	5.39	5.08	5.07	5.09	5.04	5.04

Federal Balances (Deficits):

	1995	1996	1997	1998	1999	2000	2001
Base	-173	-167	-174	-191	-220	-256	-295
New	-4	-24	-46	-82	-128	-172	-202

As in the previous case there is very little impact on gross domestic product except in this example, thanks to the modest stimulation, there is a small positive increase of a little more than $4 billion in the first year rising incrementally each year to $24.2 billion in the seventh.[9]

While one has to be a little bit skeptical of econometric simulations they do give an indication of what is possible and what is not. Personally, I think that some of the results would be a little bit better than forecast. For example, I strongly suspect that the near elimination of inflation, and consequent reduction in the cost of debt servicing, would have a more positive effect on GDP growth and federal balances than indicated. Also the GCM figures I have used may be too conservative for the fourth and subsequent years – perhaps significantly so. But even then it is painfully obvious that federal budgets will not be balanced without a subsequent increase in taxes. Increased taxes on gasoline, cigarettes and liquor, for example, could provide sufficient additional revenue to make up the shortfall. In that case there would be a substantial, one-time rise in the CPI but this would have to be "swallowed" by everyone to put the U.S. financial house in order.

The extent to which the government should use government-created money is an arbitrary decision. Personally I would have the federal government create enough to balance its budget, ab initio, and then scale back each year until the ratio of bank deposits to reserves was down to some reasonable figure like 4 to 1, or 5 to 1. After that I would split the money-creating function between the government and the banks on a 50/50 basis. That would allow the banks to meet the needs of business and increase their assets sufficiently to cover operating expenses.

A GROWTH DIVIDEND

People sometimes ask "What will make the new government-created money good? What will give it value?" In effect it will be "made good" in exactly the same way that bank-created money is made good. The existing workforce becomes a little more efficient each year through greater knowledge and the use of better capital tools. So more goods and services are produced by the same number of people. Add to that the output from additional entrants to the workforce, whether from young people growing up or from net immigration, and you have the total increase in growth of output. So the money supply can be increased in proportion to the increase in production of real goods and services without any inflationary effects as a result. That is the essence of monetarism although the theory assumes that no one will try to grab more than their fair share which is another problem to be addressed later. For the moment we will assume "fair ball" for purposes of discussion.

The principal difference between having the government print half of the new money created each year, instead of letting the banks do it all, is that the government owns part of the increase instead of the banks. You could argue that if the government gets the money (revenue), and the people make it good, that it is a form of tax. This is technically true, although I prefer to call it a growth dividend. The people finance the growth (increased output) through their government – in the role of financial intermediary – and in turn they get the benefit from the kind of services governments provide. This can be accomplished with less increase in explicit taxes which are widely regarded as high enough already. The big switch is that the people get a greater benefit from their own labor instead of working primarily for the banks which has been the over-riding result of the fractional reserve system.

The purpose of the operation is not to move to a 100% reserve system. There is no real need for theoretical purity. It is rather to increase bank reserves substantially and take away their near-monopoly on money-creation. The leverage of banks in many Western countries is positively scary and it is time to move back from the precipice of possible disaster. In addition to reducing the vulnerability of the banking system, the creation of more real money will be a move toward a safer, sounder system.

In effect it will represent a move away from such a preponderant reliance on debt in favor of a system boasting greater equity. As the volume of debt ceases to grow as rapidly, the existing debt will act as a rotating credit not too different from the way much credit is handled now. As government securities mature the proceeds will be available for re-financing. As businesses mature, and reduce their debt to equity ratios, the repayment will be available for new businesses. As people grow older, put their children through college and pay off their mortgages, the credit will be available to their children to finance the same cycle. "Crowding out" – the competition between public and private sectors for available credit – will not be affected. For every dollar the government creates it will need to borrow one dollar less. Finally, the price of money for both government and business will be more reasonable if banks are prohibited from making loans for speculative as opposed to legitimate purposes.

If this sounds like a vast improvement, it is. All that is required is a revolution of the mind.

THE CANADIAN CASE

The Canadian economy is almost a basket case, which means that much more heroic measures are required if our economy and our country are to survive. Our sad state can be traced directly to the effects of the last two horrendous recessions, compounded by the disrupting consequences of the North American Free Trade Agreement, and exacerbated by Bank of Canada interest and exchange rate policies which have been self-defeating at best and treacherous at worst.

The monetarist philosophy reigned supreme and without any of the redeeming qualities of common sense in its applica-tion. Our latest recession began ahead of the U.S., went deeper and lasted longer as our dogmatic Bank of Canada Governor, John Crow, relentlessly pursued his goal of price stability defined as zero inflation. We have achieved that goal but, as was the case with medieval doctors who bled their patients to eliminate the poison, the patient is near death's door and in need of a massive transfusion.

As the recession deepened, and government revenues declined, deficits grew larger. But instead of allowing Canadian banks to finance the deficits internally our Governor kept interest rates abnormally high and encouraged foreign banks to print the money necessary for the shortfall. As Professor W.H. Pope wrote: "Nothing is more foolish than for a country with heavy unemployment to be a net foreign borrower. All that can be done with foreign money is buy foreign goods and services and pay interest and dividends on past capital inflows."[10] Borrowing foreign money to finance government deficits, instead of financing them internally, created employment abroad and unemployment in Canada.

These foreign currencies had to be converted into Canadian dollars to buy Canadian bonds. This increased demand for the Canadian dollar and raised it to an artificially high level – so high, in fact, that our competitive position in manufactures, resources and tourism was badly eroded. Instead of allowing us to earn our way in the world, the Governor put us deeper and deeper into debt internationally to the point where foreign bankers, instead of our government, are setting public policy. To say that our present state of affairs is the result of incredibly bad judgment on the part of Mr. Crow is the most charitable way possible of accounting for it. With the patient just now, in the summer of 1994, opening an eyelid and coming out of intensive care there is no orthodox treatment that will restore the pre-operative robust health.

One additional handicap was imposed when the former Governor agreed with the government of the day that it would be permissible, in the amendments to the Bank Act in 1991, to drop the provision which allowed the cabinet to set cash reserve requirements for the chartered banks. Instead the Basle Accord, authored by the Bank for International Settlement, which merely sets "risk weighted capital requirements", was adopted. Under this system government bonds are considered "risk free" and commercial loans "100% risky". A bank must have capital equal to 8% of business loans, which are considered risky, but there is no such requirement for government bonds other than the overall limitation that total assets cannot exceed 20 times capital. If this sounds complicated, it is, but the net result is a bias in favor of government debt over business requirements. The amendment of the act was requested by the banks, sponsored by the government of the day, approved either implicitly or explicitly by the Governor of the Bank of Canada, and allowed to pass without serious debate by an opposition which was oblivious of the potentially disastrous consequences.

Having reduced inflation to near zero, Canada finally adopted a reasonable interest rate policy – nominal rates comparable to U.S. rates, though real rates were considerably higher – which had just begun to promote modest growth when the latest barrage from the Fed was launched. Monetarist policy has a very different effect in the U.S. and Canada. In the U.S. most homeowners have 15 to 30 year mortgages so if the Fed raises interest rates they are not immediately affected. The change applies primarily to those about to purchase a house and those borrowing for business activities. In Canada, a substantial proportion of home mortgages are short-term. Consequently, when interest rates go up, a huge number of people who already own homes are hit, as well as new home buyers. Thus the same monetarist policy affects consumer confidence and spending much more in Canada than in the U.S. For Canadian business loans the increase is at least tax deductible whereas for mortgages it is after tax income, which makes the hit even more drastic. (Mortgage payments are not tax-deductible in Canada.) In both countries of course, higher interest rates increase the cost of servicing government debt.

If the cash reserve requirement had remained in place the Bank of Canada could have purchased Canadian bonds to keep nominal rates from rising in concert with U.S. rates. With inflation almost 3 percentage points less than U.S. inflation, there was some maneuvring room. But the ability to pursue an independent interest-rate policy, consistent with an independent inflation policy, was effectively lost when there was no way to sterilize the massive infusion of high-powered money that would have gone into the system. As a result real Canadian long-term interest rates soared above 9 percent which is more than double what they should have been. Needless to say, the extra, unanticipated cost of servicing the debt played havoc with budgetary predictions.

The very first move Canada must take, then, is to revise the Bank Act one more time and make provision for cash reserve ratios as determined by the government or by the Bank of Canada on its behalf. Once that has been done the government will be in a position to begin the massive stimulation that is required to reduce the level of unemployment from the current 11% to something more morally and economically acceptable.

Two different types of simulations give some indication of the potential for improvement.

CANADA CASE #1

Assumptions: Figures in Cdn. $

YR.	1995	1996	1997	1998	1999	2000	2001
STIM $b.	10.0	17.5	22.5	25.0	22.5	20.0	17.5
GCM $b.	10.0	17.5	22.5	25.0	22.5	20.0	17.5

Plus Incomes Policy

As you can imagine the results from such massive stimulation are quite dramatic.

Comparison of New Policy with base case:

Unemployment:

Ref. Case	11.17	10.92	10.62	10.29	10.15	10.14	9.92
New Case	9.39	7.99	6.98	6.43	6.57	6.94	7.08

Consumer Price Index:
Year to Year Change %

Ref. Case	1.93	1.90	1.91	1.83	2.16	2.51	2.10
New Case	1.01	0.97	1.03	0.95	1.16	0.87	0.29

Gross Domestic Product:

Ref. Case $b.	614.3	634.5	652.1	669.7	685.2	699.0	715.7
New Case $b.	633.7	666.6	693.6	715.1	726.9	735.0	746.0

Federal Balances:

Ref. Case $b.	-22.1	-17.6	-14.9	-14.3	-14.0	-15.1	-15.4
New Case $b.	-17.0	-6.5	0.2	1.3	1.0	-1.1	-2.2

Case #1 is limited to increased government expenditures spread across the health-care, environmental, educational, defense and other industries and spent jointly by the federal and provincial levels of government, plus a corresponding infusion of government-created money to prevent the federal deficit from getting out of hand. The simulation included, of course, the incomes policy without which the benefits would be lost.

As you can see most of the dramatic benefits, including a balanced federal budget, occur in the first four years.[11] I suspect that the model does not fully reflect the ongoing benefits from restored confidence and rapid growth but there is no way to prove or disprove intuition except in the real world of political economy.

CANADA CASE #2

Assumptions:

YR.	1995	1996	1997	1998	1999	2000	2001
Direct STIM $b.	10.0	12.5	15.0	10.0	7.5	5.0	2.5
STIM from Elimination of GST over 3 Yrs. $b.	5.0	10.0	15.0	15.0	15.0	15.0	15.0
Total Tax & Cash STIM $b.	10.0	17.5	25.0	22.5	22.5	20.0	17.5
GCM $b.	10.0	17.5	25.0	22.5	22.5	20.0	17.5
Plus Incomes Policy							

Comparison of New Policy with base case:

Unemployment:

Ref. Case	11.17	10.92	10.62	10.29	10.15	10.14	9.92
New Case	9.39	8.17	7.01	6.84	6.92	7.19	7.23

Consumer Price:
Year to Year Change %

Ref. Case	1.90	1.90	1.91	1.83	2.16	2.51	2.10
New Case	1.00	-0.88	-1.12	-1.05	0.81	0.87	0.46

Gross Domestic Product:

Ref. Case $b.	614.4	634.5	652.1	669.7	685.2	699.0	715.7
New Case $b.	633.7	663.4	691.4	707.8	720.6	729.9	742.0

Federal Balances:

Ref. Case $b.	-22.1	-17.1	-14.9	-14.3	-14.0	-15.1	-15.4
New Case $b.	-17.0	-6.2	2.0	3.5	4.7	4.3	4.7

The second Canadian simulation is one that I vastly prefer to the first case.[12] To begin with it involves much less direct stimulation on the part of government, which is good because there is an innate tendency to be careless in the choice of expenditures when pump-priming an economy by fiscal means. Instead, a very large part of the stimulation is provided through tax elimination. This has the double benefit of reducing the extent of the trauma when the time comes that government retrenchment is called for, and putting more of the action in the private sector where it can be ongoing.

Even more important, the tax chosen to be eliminated is the much hated goods and services tax (GST), Canada's late entry into the field of value added taxes.

The advantages of this solution are quite obvious. As in Case #1, unemployment falls to 7% and the federal budget is balanced in three years. The negative inflation for three years reduces the costs of indexed pensions; but even more important the elimination of the GST would remove an irritant and stimulate tourism which is desperately needed to take some of the pressure off Canada's enormous balance of trade deficit. This is one of Canada's most intractable problems and one that has not been properly addressed. A specific and far-reaching strategy is required and part of that strategy, inevitably, must be to reduce Canada's multi-billion dollar deficit in tourism. Another plus from scrapping the GST, or minus, depending on your point of view, would be the elimination of about 5,000 govern- ment jobs directly related to its collection.

As the federal balance moved from deficit to surplus the cash available could be used for debt reduction or to reduce the level of GCM depending on the circumstances existing at the time. In Canada, unlike the U.S., the level of unemployment is so high, and the slack in the economy so great, that banks would be allowed and encouraged to make new loans to business and consumers until full employment – roughly 5% with the current disincentives to employment or about 4% if the disincentives were removed in the interim – was achieved, after which the money-creation function would be shared 50/50 with government.

CONCLUSION

A few conclusions can be reached from the U.S. and Canadian simulations. First, notwithstanding all the hokus-pokus about the Phillips Curve and the "natural" rate of unemployment, it is quite possible to achieve acceptable levels of unemployment and inflation simultaneously and for the long run. This is of primary importance! Then, with reasonable expenditure and taxation policies, it is possible to balance budgets at all levels of government. Finally, by splitting the money-creation function, the leverage of the banking system can be reduced to a sane and sound level and the worrisome upward trend in debt to GDP ratios for both governments and the economy at large capped before they become even more oppressive.

CHAPTER 8

A FALSE AND INADEQUATE DIAGNOSIS

"Economics is extremely useful as a form of employment for economists."

J.K. Galbraith

If the real economy and the hypothetical economy of the monetarist classroom were the same, there would have been no need to incorporate an incomes policy into the solution recommended in the previous chapter. Alas, monetarism as currently taught, is constructed in a vacuum. Perfect in theory, it is wicked and evil in practice, i.e. in the absence of an incomes policy.

Ironically we have the same jumping off point in Irving Fisher's quantity equation $MV = PT$, or, money multiplied by the velocity of turnover of money equals prices multiplied by the number of transactions. It says algebraically what everyone knows instinctively; there is a relation between the quantity of money on the one hand and prices on the other. It also states, by inference, that recessions and depressions have always been monetary phenomena.

One of the difficulties with a contemporary application of MV=PT is the increasingly complex and inconclusive answer to the question "What is money?" The late Professor Kenneth Boulding wrote a ditty which outlines the dilemma.

"We must have a good definition of Money,
For if we do not, then what have we got,
But a Quantity Theory of no-one-knows what,
And this would be almost too true to be funny.
Now, Banks secrete something, as bees secrete honey;
(It sticks to their fingers some, even when hot!)
But what things are liquid and what things are not,
Rests on whether the climate of business is sunny.
For both Stores of Value and Means of Exchange
Include among Assets a very wide range,
So your definition's no better than mine.
Still, with credit-card-clever computers, it's clear
That money as such will one day disappear;
Then, what isn't there we won't have to define."[1]

If Fisher's equation were an absolute truth, rather than simply a handy guide for policy makers, there would be no need to increase the money supply at all, ever. As output increased year after year prices would just decline proportionately. Stated mathematically, as output tended toward infinity, prices would tend toward zero. Everything would get cheaper each year so we wouldn't have to worry about the fact our money wages were going down, too. If we were increasingly productive, prices would decline a little bit faster than wages so our standard of living would rise.

Moving back to the real world, what young economists would be thrilled about being offered a starting salary of $40,000 a year and being told that if they worked very hard for 30 years their final salary would be around $30,000? Neither young economists nor anyone else would accept such a proposition which is too absurd for serious debate. Rather than accept lower wages most of us expect a small increase each year under normal circumstances. If those increases are as large as productivity gains – and for many years they have been larger – labor unit costs do not decline and, by extension, neither do prices.

Milton Friedman, at least, has recognized the downward stickiness of wages and prices. "'Under any conceivable institutional arrangements, and certainly under those that now prevail in the United States, there is only a limited amount of flexibility in prices and wages.' In current parlance that would certainly be called a Keynesian position."[2] So on that point he is in agreement with the late John Maynard Keynes. The difference between them is that Friedman thinks this is a bad thing and Keynes thought it was a good thing.

Whether it is a good thing or a bad thing doesn't really matter because it is a fact of life. Any economist who doesn't accept the downward stickiness of wages and prices is flying in space because he or she hasn't been exposed to the facts of life. This applies to classical, neo classical and monetarist theorists who pretend that Fisher's equation is directly applicable to the real world situation in the second half of the twentieth century. Speaking personally, I agree with Keynes because my goal is stable prices not declining prices which would wreak havoc with all fixed-interest debt instruments and labor-management agreements. I lose no sleep on this point, however, because the downward stickiness of wages and prices is so obvious that there is no point in elaborating the case. Of course there are exceptions. There are exceptions to every generality; but the exceptions are not sufficiently widespread that you can build a theory on the expectation of falling prices.

In reading "Key Propositions of Monetarism", as set out in *Monetarist Economics*, by Milton Friedman,[3] I find myself in general agreement with many of the points. These include the relation between the rate of growth of the quantity of money and the rate of growth in nominal incomes; the time lag between the rate of change in monetary growth and the rate of change in nominal incomes, etc. Where we part company completely is where Friedman asserts: "It follows from the propositions I have so far stated that *inflation is always and everywhere a monetary phenomenon* in the sense that it is and can be produced only by a more rapid increase in the quantity of money than in output. "[4] Technically true, but only a half truth in the sense that it only tells half of the story. Omission of the other half of the truth has profound implications for both theory and practice.

As the basis of his beliefs, Professor Friedman cites two U.S. experiments in the 1966-1968 period when, in a tug-of-war between fiscal and monetary policy, the latter proved to be the more formidable. He then goes on to say: "My own belief in the greater importance of monetary policy does not rest on these dramatic episodes. It rests on the experience of hundreds of years and of many countries. "[5]   I share his conviction that monetary policy is by far the most important economic tool – except in certain rare instances such as the Great Depression when it was a combination of fiscal policy and a policy of money creation by government that began to ease us out of the mess monetary policy had got us into. It was grand scale money creation by government plus grand scale government borrowing of money created by banks that got the economy moving in order to wage war. Where Friedman departs from reality is in his assumption that the economy of the second half of the twentieth century is in all material respects similar to that of the hundreds of years of experience in many countries on which he based his theory. It isn't!

The kind of "price-auction" economic model upon which monetarist theory is based never did exist in totality, although it is closer to the reality of the 19th and early 20th centuries than it is to the post World War II experience. As an incorrigible auction buff I know first-hand what a price auction looks and sounds like. I also know that sometimes there are reserve bids. In the real world there are many prices which are not flexible at all. Drop in at the post office on a slack day and see how much "elasticity" there is in the price of stamps.

It has been this inability to separate the forest from the trees that has led to some highly questionable assumptions about the cause of post-Korean War inflation. In a 1973 article entitled "Prescribing Remedies for Inflation", the late Vincent Bladen, economics professor at the University of Toronto, suggested that there are five basic causes.   In addition to monetary inflation, he mentioned government borrowing to finance wars or social programs, business expansion in excess of available savings, the cost-push of rising wages and prices, and finally a world food shortage.   If his article had been written a year later, following the dramatic increase in oil prices, no doubt he would have included that as a sixth variety.

Bladen compared the various "causes" of inflation to fever in the human body: "Just as in medicine, it is essential to identify the specific organisms causing the trouble before prescribing the antibiotic known to be effective in controlling that specific organism, so in political economy, it is essential to identify the specific variety of inflation, the specific cause of a particular inflation, before prescribing a remedy."[6]

It does seem sensible to identify the nature of an illness before prescribing a cure.   Yet one should not be misled by the medical analogy.   Inflation is inflation whether the money supply is increased to pay for wars, to finance government deficits, or to maintain a reasonable level of employment in the face of rising costs.   It is only for simplicity of analysis that I am dividing it into its two highly recognized categories: demand inflation, defined as too much money chasing too few goods, and cost-push inflation, in which costs push or chase prices (depending on which you think comes first, the chicken or the egg) to ever-higher heights in a never-ending spiral.

THE VIETNAM WAR

Monetarists, in accord with many other economists, insist that all inflation, including cost-push, has its genesis in excess demand.   The extent to which this is true is open to serious question.   The record suggests that their conclusion may be more intuitive than empirical.

In any event, most U.S. economists trace the origin of the unacceptable inflation of the 70's and early 80's to a surplus of purchasing power generated by the Vietnam War.   For example, it is Robert Lekachman's view that President Johnson's escalation of the war drained manpower from civilian

output, while "defense-generated incomes simply added themselves to other incomes in the competition for civilian goods."[7]
Congress and the White House did not drain off the excess
demand through higher taxes until 1968. Meanwhile unions
bargained, successfully, to compensate for past inflation and
to hedge against future inflation.

This opinion was endorsed by President Carter's Council
of Economic Advisers, who wrote, "It was excess aggregate
demand during the Vietnam War that drove up the underlying
rate of inflation from 1 percent to 4 or 5 percent by the end of
the 1960's."[8] Years after the fact, in his 1983 report, the Bank
of Canada Governor at that time, Gerald Bouey, climbed on that
same bandwagon.

The theory was enshrined in the 9th edition of Paul
Samuelson's textbook, *Economics*, the bible of budding
economists. Samuelson noted that "low unemployment rates
– as in the post 1965 boom, when the average dropped below
4 percent – are associated with a quickening of price inflation."[9]
This widely accepted view leaves some very large questions
unanswered. Neither Samuelson nor Lekachman has taken the
trouble to explain why even lower unemployment rates in 1952
and 1953 – the lowest in more than a quarter of a century –
were achieved without any comparable impact on prices. In
fact, the inflation curve at that time was downward.

In addition, the Vietnam theory does not explain what
happened outside the United States. If Governor Bouey was
correct when he said "demand pressures showed up first in the
United States, largely associated with the Vietnam War, and
later elsewhere,"[10] how does he account for the fact that wages
and prices began their steep ascent in Canada and the United
Kingdom a year or so before they did in the United States?[11]
Neither country was significantly affected by American involvement in Southeast Asia; therefore to conform with the
conventional wisdom their surge in prices should have followed
rather than preceded the one in America.

DEMAND SHOCKS

The "It started with Vietnam" school has been extended into a general theory in an attempt to explain the ratchet-like escalation of prices over the fifteen-year period from 1965 to 1980. The Vietnam War is now cited as the first of three major events that caused the rate of inflation to surge upward.

In his final *Economic Report to Congress*, Jimmy Carter said the second, which came in the early 1970's, "was associated with the first massive oil-price increase, a worldwide crop shortage which drove up food prices, and an economy which again became somewhat overheated in 1972 and 1973. The third inflationary episode came in 1979 and 1980. It was principally triggered by another massive oil-price increase, but part of the rise in inflation may also have been due to overall demand in the economy pressing on available supply."[12]

All well and good. No one denies that each of the three shock-waves affected prices. But President Carter went on to explain that "late in each of the three inflationary episodes monetary and fiscal restraints were applied, and at the end of each a recession took place, with rising unemployment and idle capacity."[13] On the basis of classical theory, as well as of Newton's law of gravitation, prices should then have come down to the previous levels. They had adjusted on innumerable occasions in earlier decades, so why not now?

President Carter's hindsight was dead on when he observed: "A set of inflationary causes raises the rate of inflation; when the initiating factors disappear, inflation does not recede to its starting position despite the occurrence of recession; the wage-price spiral then tends to perpetuate itself at a new and higher level .... It is this downward insensitivity of inflation in the face of economic slack that has given the last 15 years their inflationary bias."[14] What he didn't explain is where the "downward insensitivity" came from.

In reviewing Presidents' reports for those years, and those of their economic advisers, I found periodic temporary shortages of various goods that would explain why an increase in price would occur. I was unable to unearth examples, with the possible exception of energy, where the shortage was sufficiently prolonged to sustain a permanent price rise. Consequently, I find the demand-shock theory, in isolation, untenable.

In rejecting the Vietnam and demand-shock theses, I wish to underline that I am not speaking of other days and other times. The demand inflation generated as an aftermath of war is well documented.[15] Today, however, this is not a relevant factor. World War II and Korea are distant memories, and any effects from the Vietnam War, which were probably overstated, have long since dissipated.

GOVERNMENT DEFICITS

Another frequently cited scapegoat for inflation is government deficits.   A group of prominent Canadian economists, in a letter to the Prime Minister in December 1975, stated that of three domestic causes of inflation, "first is the growth in government deficits: federal, provincial and municipal."[16] The same opinion is held by many American businessmen and economists.   In "Causes and Effects of Inflation," C. Lowell Harriss states that "federal deficits are widely assumed to be a source, perhaps the chief source, of inflation."[17]

This widespread belief is milked to advantage by political parties of all stripes in opposition. Especially for conservatives, everywhere, the "evil" of big budgetary deficits is accepted as faithfully as holy writ. Nevertheless, as Harriss went on to say: "Such a conclusion is not necessarily accurate. The Federal Reserve faces no legal or economic compulsion to provide the banking system with extra reserves so that banks can create money (deposits) to buy the additions to federal debt. The Treasury may go into the capital markets, and by borrowing there, reduce the amounts available for utilities, housing, manufacturing, and other borrowers."[18]

President Reagan's Council of Economic Advisers tacitly acknowledged this distinction in their 1982 report. "The impact of a specific deficit will vary, however, depending on the

conditions that lead to it. For example, during a recession –
as now exists – the borrowing requirements of business and
consumers tend to be relatively small. At such a time a given
deficit can be financed with less pressure on interest rates than
during a period of growth, when business and consumer
demands for credit are increasing. That is why it is important
for the government to reduce the budget deficit in fiscal 1983
and beyond, a period of anticipated rapid economic growth
when private investment demands are expected to rise substantially."[19]

Ironically, the monetarist approach to inflation fighting
is incompatible with fiscal conservatism. "During the last year,
(1981) better-than-expected progress on inflation has reduced
taxable income, slowing the growth of revenues below earlier
projections. The recession has temporarily slowed the growth
of the tax base while increasing outlays for employment-related
programs."[20] So to the extent that deficits are really inflationary, much of what has been gained on the monetary swing has
been lost on the fiscal roundabout. An analysis of the consequences of the 1981-82 and 1990-91 recessions demonstrates
that nothing contributes more directly and more dramatically
to an increase in government deficits than the abrupt decline in
revenues caused by inflation fighting through monetary means.

There are economists who doubt that deficits have been
a major contributor to inflation. In Canada the conventional
wisdom was effectively challenged by Robert B. Crozier when
he was senior economist for the Conference Board of Canada.
In a 1976 study entitled *Deficit Financing and Inflation: Facts
and Fictions* [21] Crozier showed that, in Canada, deficit financing
had been a negligible factor contributing to inflation. What had
been more important was the increasing proportion of total output spent by governments. The high taxes required to finance
these expenditures added considerably to unit costs both
directly, as a significant element in prices, and indirectly, by
increasing labor demands for higher wages. Thus government
expenditures have been an important contributor to cost-push
(or tax-push, as some people like to call it) inflation.

Jimmy Carter's advisers entered a note of caution on the same subject: "If government budget deficits are the cause of inflation, it should make no difference whether the deficit occurs at the Federal, State or local level .... The combined budgets of Federal, State and local governments have either showed a surplus or a really small deficit during the past two decades, except during recessions and for two years when Federal spending on the Vietnam War was at its peak.

"This notion that budget deficits are the chief cause of inflation also founders on the comparison of budget deficits and inflation among different countries. Japan and Germany in recent years have had much better success in combating inflation than the United States. Yet their budget deficits, especially those of Japan, have been much higher relative to the size of their economies than has been the case in the United States."[22]

I have long been convinced that budget deficits are neither the sole nor principal cause of contemporary inflation in Western industrialized economies. There is much evidence to support my conclusion. That said, it doesn't follow that the size of the deficit is unimportant. It depends, as a politician might say, on the circumstances.

Reagan's Council of Economic Advisers made the categorical assertion that "it is now generally agreed that continued excessive growth in the money supply will cause sustained inflation. Thus, deficits financed by money creation will have persistent inflationary consequences."[23] The second half of the statement is true only in the context of the preamble where the operative word is "excessive". If the growth in the money supply is excessive there will be inflation with or without deficits. If the expansion of the money stock is not excessive the impact of the deficit will depend, as Lowell Harriss suggested, on where the money to make up the shortfall comes from. One has to look at the total expansion of the money supply, and the use to which it is put, in order to evaluate the impact of deficit financing.

If a government increases its deficit to buy another car for the police, the net effect would be the same as if an individual borrowed the same amount of money to acquire a vehicle for his or her own private use. That said, in both cases the impact on the economy would depend on whether the automobile industry was already operating at capacity.

I accept Harriss' conclusion: "If the economy has much unutilized productive capacity, money creation may finance benefits from government spending without loss of either output or price level increases."[24] If, on the other hand, the capacity of the economy is fully utilized, printing more money will be inflationary regardless of whether the extra cash is used for public or private purposes.

THE ENERGY CRISIS

Another diagnosis attributes inflation to the effects of the rapid escalation of oil prices. The world price of oil soared from $3.00 to $11.65 a barrel between October 1, 1973, and January 1, 1974, resulting in American consumer price increases of 75.5 percent for gasoline and motor oil, 247.5 percent for fuel oil and coal, and 40.6 percent for gas and electricity.[25]

Former Treasury Secretary William E. Simon told a Senate Sub-Committee on September 8, 1974, that "the quadrupling of oil prices over the past year, when its effects are fully felt, will have contributed in the range of 5 to 8 percentage points in our wholesale price index." He added that this was about half the increase in the index for the year ending mid-1974.[26] Later statistics put the effects of the oil-price rise in better perspective. Joel Popkin, a staff member of the President's Council of Economic Advisers, said that energy prices to consumers increased 33.5 percent in the year after the cost of imported oil shot upward, while consumer prices as a whole jumped 11.2 percent. Popkin estimated that energy was responsible for just under one-fifth of the increase in the cost of living.[27]

In Canada, where the increase in oil prices was controlled, the energy component of inflation was even less. Conference Board of Canada analysts estimated that, on average, energy contributed about one-tenth of the increase in the Consumer Price Index for the 1975-81 period. Still, politicians used the actions of the oil cartel as an excuse for the inflation they didn't understand and seemed powerless to control. In his January 1980 Report to Congress, President Carter cited oil prices as "the major reason for the worldwide speed-up in inflation during 1979 and the dimming of growth prospects for 1980."[28]

By 1982 the worm had turned. Increased output by non-OPEC countries, including Britain, Norway, and Mexico, combined with slack demand due to conservation measures and the world-wide recession, created an oil glut. Prices turned soft and by the end of the year were exerting downward pressure on the Consumer Price Index.[29]

At an extended meeting in March 1983 the OPEC ministers finally came to grips with the new reality and agreed to an official reduction of $5 a barrel to bring their prices in line with the new world oil price. Today, in 1994, they have difficulty in agreeing on anything. Consequently world oil prices have been trending first downward and then up again. They are not, however, a major factor in consumer price indices.

Reflecting on the impact of oil prices in the 1970's, one might indeed ask why some countries were so much more successful than others. West Germany and Switzerland both import a higher proportion of their oil needs than do the United States and Canada. It would follow that if oil was the major disrupting factor on economic performance, their records should have been poorer than ours. In fact, they were much better.

For a time when the oil-producing and exporting countries had their act together the whole world shook, yet statistics show that the cartel was given far too much blame for a problem that has been, for the most part, domestic in origin.

EXPECTATIONS

Expectations is a mutant of the rational expectations theory and of all explanations for inflation it is the most airy-fairy and mercurial. But like most ideas, it is not without a germ of truth. Beginning about 1970 when the wage-price spiral began to spin faster and faster, nearly everyone expected, on the basis of what was happening, that the process would continue. So wages and prices began to leap-frog as management and labor anticipated the actions of the other. It was the first time since the Korean War that prices had not followed wages and represented a rational adjustment by business to labor's expected behavior. Both sides had their sails trimmed with the imposition of the 1981-82 credit squeeze but none of this explains why they were sailing above the limit in the first place.

Similarly, one can argue that rising interest rates in 1994 reflect a rational expectation that the Fed cannot guarantee low inflation except for brief periods every ten years or so when it applies the monetary guillotine. Owners of wealth tack on a premium, especially on long-term paper, as a consequence of their disbelief. None of this explains why the Fed, armed with its monetarist philosophy and natural rate of unemployment, cannot achieve price stability. It has not in the past, so rational expectations say that it will not and probably cannot in the future. It is rational, therefore, not to believe them, based on performance.

PASSING THE BUCK

Finally, when all else fails and economists still feel uneasy about their analyses of contemporary inflation, they take refuge in the popular notion that it is an international problem largely beyond the competence of individual nation states. They argue that the world economy has become so interdependent that it rises and falls like the tides. Any one country is like a cork on the surface, unable to influence its own movement.

The theory is expounded in the Mundell-Laffer Hypothesis.[30] Rather than view the United States or any other economy as closed, with international relationships grafted on, these two economists insist that the only closed economy it makes sense to talk about is the world economy. One cannot understand the U.S. economy from an American perspective; it must be viewed from a global perspective.

Certainly no country is an island unto itself. A severe frost in the coffee plantations of Brazil affects the world-wide price of the aromatic bean. A similar freeze in Florida boosts the price of orange juice in both Canada and the United States. A major wheat shortage in Russia or China influences the market for grain in North America just as surely as does a crop failure at home. A sudden disappearance of the anchovy off the coast of South America creates unforeseen and far-reaching effects on soy-bean prices in the American Midwest.

It is also true that actions in the monetary field in one powerful jurisdiction affect the ability of other countries to pursue an independent course. Excessively high interest rates in Germany have a disruptive effect on economic performance all across Europe as well as on interest rates world-wide. Any gyration in the U.S. price of money lands on Canadian shores with gale force and devastating effect. Canadian vulnerability has been exacerbated by a 1991 revision to the Bank Act which has now eliminated the necessity for cash reserves in the banking system. This robbed the Bank of Canada of its most powerful tool for pursuing a somewhat independent interest rate course based on our very low inflation. The bankers stole our ammunition before the battle began.

As Mundell and Laffer point out, there is evidence that prices, including the price of money, tend to seek a world level. But it is also true that some countries have a much better record in matters of employment and price stability than others and there has been no satisfactory explanation given for these significant variations from the norm.

I admit that no country with an open economy can prevent changes of individual prices affected by world markets. But that doesn't explain or excuse a general rise in prices when the price of oil, lumber, or food goes up. In a free market, with a fixed money supply, some prices must fall when others rise. When people have only so much money to spend and they decide to spend more for one item, then, automatically, they must spend less on something else. Demand for the other item or items declines, and prices should fall accordingly. Consequently, any country in control of its own currency should be able to maintain a constant average price level – at least in theory.

Gerald Bouey, when he was Governor of the Bank of Canada, almost made that point in his 1980 report where he said: "I do not regard increases in the price of one commodity, relevant to another, as a valid reason for a general acceleration of the rate of inflation, because in a less inflationary environment faster-than-average increases in some prices would tend to be offset by slower-than-average increases in others."[31]

If it isn't necessary for the rate of inflation to increase when one price goes up, as the Governor maintained, then by the same logic it should be possible to maintain stable prices. When some prices go up, others should come down. That is how the system should work and would work if we really had a pure market economy. Still, the professionals trot out increases in one commodity as justification for a general price rise. They refuse to admit that we haven't had, don't have, and never will have a "pure" market economy. They just keep pretending that black and gray are white.

CHAPTER 9

THE SCHIZO ECONOMY

"Both parties join'd to do their best to damn the public interest. "

Samuel Butler

Modern industrial economies are a mixture of small and large, public and private enterprise where some prices are determined by the law of supply and demand and others, including some of the most important ones, are not. Price-competitive enterprise operates side by side with natural monopolies, oligopolies, and trade unions which restrict the market in labor and render prices inelastic. A system comprising both free and rigid sectors can be labeled a schizo economy – one where two very different kinds of enterprise must co-exist.

Although natural monopolies play a significant role in the economy, their power and overall economic impact are minimal in comparison to that of the oligopolies – the inelegant name that economists have applied to situations where the market is dominated by a few sellers. Any progressive concentration of market power is likely to end in oligopoly. Important concentrations have occurred in many industries. Markets for

124

cereal breakfast foods, cookies and crackers, chocolate and cocoa products, chewing gum, malt beverages, roasted coffee, cigarettes, pet food, soaps and detergents, explosives, industrial gases, distilled and blended liquors, tires and tubes, gypsum products, flavoring extracts and syrups, sanitary paper products, knit underwear, womens hosiery and myriad other products are dominated by a handful of firms. More than 50 percent of sales accrue to four or fewer companies.[1]

The fact that the concentration has not continued to the point where oligopoly is replaced by monopoly is a benefit that University of Chicago economist and Nobel laureate George Stigler attributes to antitrust laws. He argues that antitrust policies have replaced monopoly and incipient monopoly with oligopoly as the dominant industrial market structure.[2] In *The Economics of Antitrust, Competition and Monopoly*, Richard E. Low says: "This argument can be supported by a host of historical evidence. Oil, tobacco, steel and many other leading products were produced by monopolies, or near monopolies in the early part of this century, until these monopolies were dissolved by the application of antitrust suits or by the passage of time. According to Professor Stigler, and he seems to have logic on his side, time proved as effective as it did only because of the ever-present threat of antitrust. The power of monopolies and of cartels in modern economies without our antitrust policies substantiates this belief."[3]

Whether the difference between U.S. and European experience has been due to the threat of antitrust's big stick or the relative size of the markets is immaterial to most economists' belief that the oligopolies' record in pricing, output, and economic progress is far better than that of monopolies. Even so, that is not to say that they normally engage in the kind of price competition that occurs when there are many sellers. They are far too interdependent.

Professor Richard E. Caves's description of oligopoly underscores the importance of this seller interdependence. "The essence of oligopoly is that firms are few enough to recognize the impact of their actions on their rivals and thus on the market as a whole.... When an industry contains one firm (monopoly) or many firms (pure competition), the individual sellers react only to impersonal market forces. In oligopoly they react to one another in a direct and personal fashion. This inevitable interaction of sellers in an oligopolistic market we call mutual interdependence. Where mutual interdependence exists, sellers do not just take into account the effects of their actions on the total markets ... they also take into account the effects of their actions on one another. Oligopoly becomes something like a poker game."[4]

It is a game in which the stakes are too high to engage in predatory price-cutting. This rule is so entrenched that oligopolists seldom break it. When they do – as in the case of the U.S. steel industry in 1982, or the tobacco industry in 1993 – the self-immolation is so painful that it doesn't take long for reason to return. Or, if it doesn't, pressure is likely to be applied by what John R. Munkirs calls the Central Planning Committee of the U.S. In his book *The Transformation of American Capitalism From Competitive Market Structures to Centralized Private Sector Planning*, Munkirs asserts that all of America's largest corporations are indirectly controlled and directed by seven large banks and five large insurance companies through a network of interlocking directorships representing either debt or equity interest in the company.[5] Heaven help any chief executive officer who pits his power against theirs.

Normally, oligopolists play according to their own tacitly understood set of rules and limit competition to advertising and promotion, style changes, and product improvement. This well-understood practice was confirmed for me some years ago by a senior executive of one of the big soap companies. At a luncheon following a seminar on the subject, one of his subordinates had been dutifully denying the remotest possibility of cooperation among companies. His chief, who didn't wish to appear ridiculous in the face of a convincing case, merely said, "Let's say we have an understanding."

Of course they do. Oligopolists do not write memoranda of agreement to set prices. They just reach an understanding over tea. Their costs rise at roughly the same rate, so their prices rise to about the same level at approximately the same time. That is quite natural and oligopolies are very good at doing what comes naturally.

LABOR

If the existence of natural monopolies and oligopolies chips away at the free-market illusion, the power and influence of the trade union movement undermine its very foundation. Combine the power of unions with that of oligopolistic and monopolistic employers and the whole concept of free-market price determination falls in ruins.

From the small, struggling craft unions the movement has grown to the point where it qualifies in its own right as big business. Not only do unions handle enormous sums of money for current operations, strike funds, and pensions, they have gained sufficient political clout to make politicians tremble. Even more important, from an economic point of view, big unions have become monopoly suppliers of labor in many of the big industries.

According to Harvard economists Richard Freeman and James Medoff, "Most, if not all, unions have monopoly power, which they can use to raise wages above competitive levels."[6] The power of unions to raise wages in excess of market levels is derived from privileges that have been extended by government through statutes, regulations and non-enforcement of other laws. In many jurisdictions it is an exceedingly powerful advantage. Ludwig van Mises, an economist who was not sympathetic to labor, wrote in 1922, "The long and short of trade union rights is in fact the right to proceed against the strikebreaker with primitive violence."[7] In some jurisdictions, like the Canadian provinces of Quebec and Ontario, strike-breaking is prohibited by law.

As a member of the Alliance of Canadian Cinema, Television and Radio Artists (ACTRA) I am not unfriendly to the legitimate aims and aspirations of labor. On the contrary! But as I told my good friend Shirley Carr, former president of the Canadian Labour Congress (Canada's equivalent to the U.S.

AFL/CIO), being a union member doesn't take away my right to think. What is widely known as free collective bargaining can be, and often is, free collective blackmail and the results of its use are often detrimental to both the long-term interests of the workers involved and of their fellow citizens.

The consequences for the economy at large are monumental. Businesses are directly affected by the actions of their competitors. One generous settlement can create shock-waves for the whole industry, and it matters little whether the award is related to productivity or simply the vulnerability of the target company. It's a phenomenon that a number of economists, including Aubrey Jones, a former Tory cabinet minister, and later Wages and Prices Commissioner under a Labour government in the United Kingdom, have dubbed "wage leadership."[8] The most powerful union, in the most strategically advantageous position, sets the yardstick by which all subsequent negotiations are measured.

The practice is widespread in industrialized societies. *Wage Inflation and Wage Leadership: A Study of the Role of Key Wage Bargains in the Irish System of Collective Bargaining*, by W.E.J. McCarthy, J.F. O'Brien and V.G. Dowd, underlines its significance in that country. "One of the most important conclusions to emerge is that wage leadership could give rise to rapidly rising prices even if all other factors contributing to the latter process were totally neutralized. This is so because key wage claims, induced by disturbed relativities, can initiate a general upward movement in wages which has no justification whatever beyond the restoration of initial wage relativities. This vital point has never been explicitly brought out in the substantial body of statistical, economic and econometric work which has already been published concerning inflation in Ireland. The principal reason for this is that these disciplines cannot cope with the institutional dynamics which lie at the heart of the problem."[9]

That is the nut of it. The science of economics has no mathematical formula to quantify a phenomenon that is as much political and sociological as economic. A phenomenon, nevertheless, with incalculable economic consequences.

The impact from the unregulated exercise of monopoly union power has not yet been incorporated into the economic equation.   This results in some strange anomalies.   For example, natural monopolies have their prices to consumers regulated; yet one of their principal costs is not.   So wage increases, no matter how great, are just passed through to the consuming public.

I recall a former president of Bell Telephone of Canada – a monopoly at the time – vehemently insisting that big business was responsible enough to police its own labor settlements in a manner compatible with the public interest.   Only weeks later his company signed a pace-setting agreement in order to avoid a strike.   Naturally, Bell was allowed to pass the highly inflationary cost increases on to its subscribers without penalty.   Not only that, the magnitude of the settlement became a bench-mark for divers service unions.

In practice, oligopolies have often been pretty much in the same boat as monopolies – although that is certainly less so today than it was a decade ago.   To the extent that they have the collective market power to pass cost increases on to the consuming public, they are less responsible in policing their own settlements.   Like big labor, big business puts its own perceived short-term interests first.   Consequently, many contracts are signed that appear beneficial to business or labor or both but may be detrimental to the public interest.

Whether by monopolies, oligopolies or governments, it has been the approval of wage increases well in excess of average productivity that led inexorably to an ever higher-level of underlying inflation.   Each additional increase, whether in response to higher oil prices, more expensive food, or just a desire to keep up with a new record settlement, gave the spiral another twist.

WAGES OUT OF JOINT WITH PRODUCTIVITY

For more than a quarter of a century I have argued that the principal cause of contemporary inflation in Western industrialized economies is nominal wage increases being out-of-joint with productivity. Oil shocks and other price changes produce blips but the trend line is determined by the gap between nominal wages and real output.

Most economists recognize that there is a relationship between wages and prices. The President's Council of Economic Advisers was right on target in its 1981 report in saying: "... since payments to labor are estimated to account for almost two-thirds of total production costs, prices over the long term tend to move in conjunction with changes in labor unit costs."[10]

Precisely! In the longer term, prices move up at a rate that approximates the increase in wages and fringe benefits minus the increase in real output per person.

CONTEMPORARY INFLATION: $\dot{P} = \dot{W} - \dot{Q}$

The data support the proposition as closely as anything in economics. The rate of change in the price level will approximate the difference between the average rate of change in money wages, including fringe benefits, and the average rate of change in the production of goods and services. Stating this symbolically, we have $\dot{P} = \dot{W} - \dot{Q}$ where $\dot{P}$ is the rate of change in the price level, $\dot{W}$ is the average rate of change in money wages, and $\dot{Q}$ is the average rate in real output of goods and services per worker in the labor force.

The assumptions include reasonable levels of employment. The definition varies from country to country, but for my purposes it is the condition that would be considered "normal" at the time. Another condition is a neutral monetary policy. This assumes that the money stock will be changed at a rate that will neither "overheat" nor "cool" the economy. The third assumption is that domestic prices are not unduly influenced by imports - that in fact import prices are rising at a rate more or less comparable to domestic prices.

Of course $\dot{P} = \dot{W} - \dot{Q}$ is an imprecise formula – especially in the short run - because its accuracy depends on assumptions that seldom apply for extended periods. But if one looks at the data for a group of fifteen O.E.C.D. (Organization for Economic Co-operation and Development) countries shown in Table 1 the long-term result for most countries is close. The over-all average of averages is amazingly accurate – within one-quarter of one percent over a 27 year period.[11] A correlation that close is very convincing!

Table 1

Average Growth Rates of
Prices, Wages, and Productivity for 15 O.E.C.D. Countries
(W,Q calculated per Member of the Labour Force), 1964-1991

	(1) P	(2) W	(3) Q	(4) W-Q	(5) (1)-(4)
Austria	4.3	7.7	3.0	4.7	-0.4
Belgium	5.0	7.7	2.6	5.1	-0.1
Canada	5.6	7.1	1.3	5.8	-0.2
Denmark	6.6	8.5	1.5	7.0	-0.4
France	6.3	9.2	2.5	6.7	-0.4
Germany	3.3	6.4	2.4	4.0	-0.7
Ireland	8.2	11.3	3.3	8.0	0.2
Italy	8.5	11.9	2.9	9.0	-0.5
Japan	5.2	9.5	4.4	5.1	0.1
Netherlands	4.6	6.3	1.5	4.8	-0.2
Norway	6.6	8.3	2.3	6.0	0.6
Sweden	6.9	8.9	1.7	7.2	-0.3
Switzerland	3.9	6.4	1.5	4.9	-1.0
U.K.	7.7	9.4	1.8	7.6	0.1
U.S.A.	5.2	6.0	0.8	5.2	0.0
Aggregate Average	5.85	8.29	2.23	6.07	-0.22

Source: Q,W - OECD National Accounts;
P=CPI in IMF Financial Statistics Yearbook
Labour Force - OECD Labour Force Statistics

It may be of interest to note that this is the fourth time that I have had this table prepared for various periods beginning in 1958 and the correlation has always been of the same order of magnitude.

THE FATAL FLAW

The failure to recognize the primary role of wage increases in excess of productivity as the principal initiator of inflation since the system settled down after the Korean War has been the fatal flaw in economic theory and, by extension, public policy. Monetarists like Milton Friedman have recognized that the market for labor has been altered by legislation and regulation. In his book *Free to Choose*, where he discusses how the labor market operates, he says: "Here, too, interference by government, through minimum wages, for example, or trade unions, through restricting entry, may distort the information transmitted or may prevent individuals from freely acting on that information"[12]

Quite so! But having observed and objected to the rigidities in the labor market due to government intervention, he proceeds to ignore the connection between wages and prices by denying the existence of cost-push inflation. He pretends that the system is self-regulating and that equilibrium will be restored by some invisible hand. Yet even after two disastrous recessions and one inadequate recovery since *Free to Choose* was written, the kind of free market he dreams of and writes about does not exist. Nor will it in his lifetime or mine.

The Friedman analysis of where capitalism went wrong and his conclusion that business cycles were caused by monetary excesses is exactly what I believe. His concern that governmental intervention has reached the point where it actually impedes the satisfaction of human needs strikes a sympathetic cord and is consistent with my experience in the business world. But his solution to the problem of contemporary inflation is one that ignores the rigidities that he deplores. For him labor is just another price freely determined in the market.

This blind spot has been noted by many critics. In *Capitalism's Inflation and Unemployment Crisis*, Sidney Weintraub says: "To interpret money wages as 'simply another price' is to mistake flies for elephants." A general wage rise "comprises about 55 percent of gross business costs, closer to

75 percent of net costs, and probably even more of variable costs."[13] In fact, money wages constitute the major factor in the economic equation; they far outshadow any other price.

In view of this, one should not underestimate the significance of Dr. Friedman's unsubstantiated contention that "wage increases in excess of increases in productivity are a result of inflation rather than the cause."[14] This proposition appears to fly in the face of the data. The Organization for Economic Co-operation and Development (OECD) Main Economic Indicators show that wages outstripped productivity in the United States every year from 1964 to 1991. Therein lies the principal source of the inflation for that period.

Not only have wages moved up faster than productivity from at least as far back as 1958, they outpaced prices in 18 of the 21 years – the exceptions being '70, '74 and '79 – prior to the time Milton and Rose Friedman first published *Free to Choose* in 1980. The wage index for the entire period up to the present – of which the 1964-1991 segment can be seen in Figure 6 – has kept well ahead of the price index.

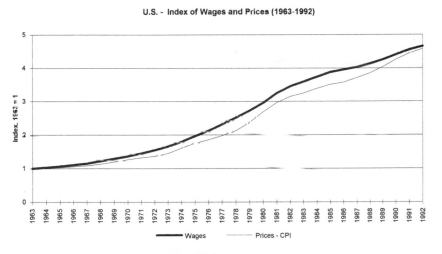

U.S. - Index of Wages and Prices (1963-1992)

Figure 6

Source: International Financial Statistics Yearbook 1993, IMF.

Disagreement concerning the origin of the wage-price spiral is exceeded only by apparent uncertainty as to which came first, the chicken or the egg. Businessmen know which came first. Anyone who has made or sold a product or marketed a service knows that pricing begins by adding up the costs, including labor, and then adding a margin of profit. When the cost of labor rises faster than productivity, prices must rise. There are cases where a brisk demand may permit a higher markup or a slack demand may dictate a lower one; but inevitably the pricing mechanism begins by covering costs. Published data show that this is the sequence.

The following five graphs for the United States, Canada, Germany, the United Kingdom and Japan illustrate clearly that wages led prices almost exclusively. The few exceptions apply primarily in the United States and only after the monetarist counter-revolution had captured the hearts and minds of many theorists - which should provide them with scant solace. In fact price increases seldom if ever exceeded wage increases until stagflation became the dominant aspect of the system. Then both business and labor were anticipating inflationary increases and attempts were made to leap-frog the process.

United States: Wages and Prices (1956-1992)

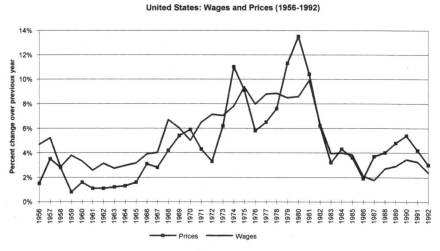

Figure 7

Source: International Financial Statistics Yearbook, 1993, IFM.

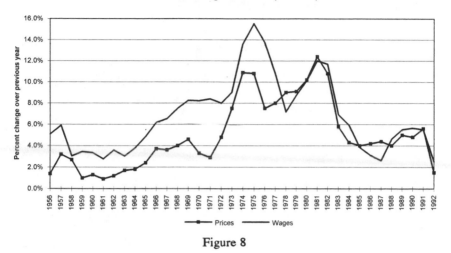

Figure 8

Source: International Financial Statistics Yearbook, 1993, IFM.

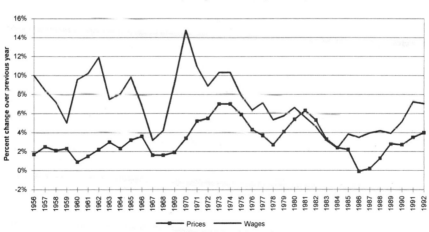

Figure 9

Source: International Financial Statistics Yearbook, 1993, IFM.

United Kingdom: Wages and Prices (1956-1992)

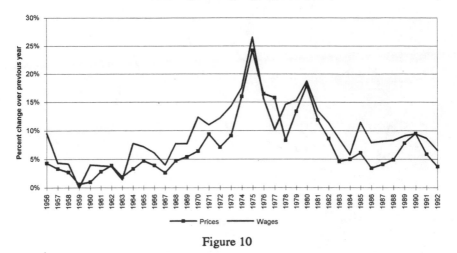

Figure 10

Source: International Financial Statistics Yearbook, 1993, IFM.

Japan: Wages and Prices (1956-1992)

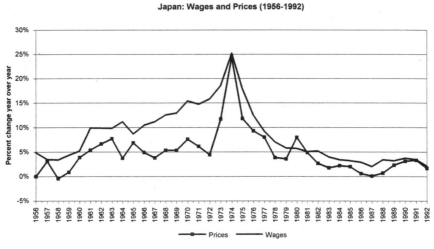

Figure 11

Source: International Financial Statistics Yearbook, 1993, IFM.

MONETARISM + MONOPOLY POWER = STAGFLATION

With both classical and monetarists economists either being unable to recognize or refusing to admit the predominant initiator of contemporary inflation, it is little wonder that official policy, based largely on their prescriptions, has been so disappointing at best and disastrous at worst. Attempts to control wage-push inflation by monetary means have been made at least six times since I first entered public life and always with the same results. The inflation rate has fallen but at the expense of employment and output. Eventually, when the rate of unemployment reached the political flash point, the monetary authorities have relaxed the system, lowered interest rates, and allowed the economy to expand and create more jobs. Each time the operation began the impression was given that the action taken would produce a permanent cure. But it never did! The end of one cycle simply marked the beginning of the next. That is the reason that despite my promise that there would only be two equations in this book I decided to be generous and throw in a third by asserting that monetarism plus monopoly power equals stagflation. It has for the last two decades, it does now and it will as long as the two protagonists – monetarists and monopoly power – are locked in combat.

When earlier attempts failed to change "inflationary expectations", the fraternity of central bankers decided that they would prescribe a massive dose of the same old medicine and carry the experiment to its logical conclusion – presumably price stability. In discussing the Fed's approach of reducing the rate of growth in the monetary aggregates in 1980, Chairman Paul Volcker used a distinctly monetarist-like formulation. "Our policy, taken in a longer perspective, rests on a simple premise – documented by centuries of experience – that the inflationary process is ultimately related to excessive growth in money and credit."[15] So he, along with Governor Gerald Bouey in Canada, and other central bankers, put the monetary machine into a nose dive. So steep was its descent that they just managed to level out in time to prevent the collapse of the whole Western monetary system. In the meantime the human and economic fallout was astronomical. Business bankruptcies soared, thousands of people lost their homes because they couldn't afford to pay the interest on their mortgages, thousands lost their farms, sometimes after several generations in the family, and the total level of unemployment in the Western world reached 30 million. Shame! At the same time, as Figure 12 shows, interest crowded out other forms of income.

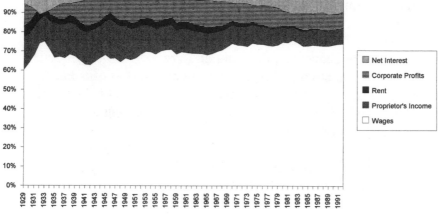

Figure 12

Source: U.S. National Income and Product Accounts

To continue the medical analogy, you would think that after a disease recurs two, three, or four times and the medicine prescribed creates side-effects far worse than the disease itself, policy makers would demand either a new doctor or a new prescription. Not so, an interval of about 10 years was allowed to go by before the decision was made to administer another massive dose of the same poison. It goes without saying that we have suffered the same kind of disastrous consequences in other areas including an increase in crime, an increase in family violence and breakup, and a higher suicide rate of which part, at least, can easily be attributable to the economic malaise and its resulting sense of hopelessness.

Not only did the two great recessions of the 80's and 90's produce what any civilized society should consider unacceptable consequences on the human side, the loss in government revenues attributable to the economic slow-down resulted in larger deficits and more debt. It is easy for central bankers to get up on their soap boxes and blame the whole mess on the fiscal irresponsibility of politicians. But that is not the whole truth – just a semblance of it. The political system is not geared to slash programs and benefits as fast as revenues fall from deliberately induced monetary recessions. Consequently politicians' hands are tied by a situation over which they have little, if any, control. The marked increase in U.S. debt relative to Gross Domestic Product, which began with the 1981-82 recession, is dramatized in Figure 13. Other countries have been subject to similar increases from which there appears to be no hope of escape.

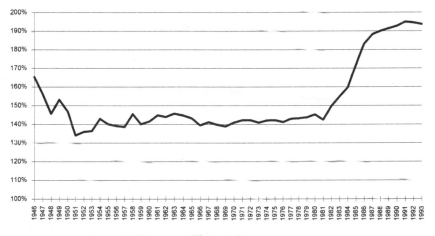

U.S. - Total Nonfinancial Credit Market Debt as a percent of GDP (1946-1993)

Figure 13

Source: Flow of Funds Accounts Financial Assets and Liabilities Year End, Tables L2 - L4, U.S. Federal Reserve System.

In 1994 we stand on the threshold of another disaster. The Fed has been so concerned about the prospect of a little economic growth that they started to put water on the fire when the flames had only been visible through the dampened coals for a few months. Why? There is something structurally wrong with a system where the financial community kicks the economy in the shins as soon as it appears to be gaining strength. Rising interest rates have unsettled markets and applied the economic brakes long before the rate of unemployment dropped to a level which can be called morally acceptable. Implicitly, at least, the Fed is opting for continuous high unemployment and limited inflation – i.e. stagflation.

If the classical trade-off were the only option available, one would have to closely examine the morality of following a policy which consistently favors the rich at the expense of the poor and the unemployed. Hopefully clearer heads will prevail and realize there is another option. The introduction of an incomes policy, which will prevent a recurrence of wage-push inflation, will allow the Fed to tolerate a much higher rate of growth for a longer period and, in effect, to finance full employment and maximum output for years to come. Policy makers who have the best interests of their constituents at heart should take little time in adopting the medicine appropriate to the disease.

CHAPTER 10

AN INCOMES POLICY FOR MONOPOLIES AND OLIGOPOLIES

"All the forces in the world are not as powerful as an idea whose time has come."

Victor Hugo

In order to be effective an incomes policy for the control of monopoly power must create a climate in which the economic system will work well all of the time instead of just some of the time. Specifically, the goal is to permit the achievement of full employment and stable prices simultaneously and for an extended period.

This is where monetarism has failed. It has an incomes policy aspect to the extent that it is designed to slow down or stop excessive wage and price gains. Unfortunately, its means of doing so is cruel and inefficient. Despite the damage caused by its policies, price stability has never been achieved! Also, to the extent it has been responsible for reducing inflation, this has never been for an extended period. Of the many incomes policies I have looked at, including earlier American and Canadian experiments, monetarism is, unquestionably, the worst!

I am in total agreement with the goal of price stability. Eliminating inflation is critically important because any inflation is too much. Inflation is a form of larceny. It robs one group of people (lenders) for the benefit of another group (borrowers). If I thought that "hard money" could only be achieved at the expense of the poor and the unemployed, then my vote would be for the disadvantaged, as I have noted in the last chapter. But it is my belief that the trade-off theory, in the extremes to which it is widely accepted, is as phony as a $3 bill.

Certainly there is a level of unemployment at which demand for labor would begin to increase the price. But that is not the same level which would trigger higher union demands in contract negotiations in the course of an economic recovery. The latter is a much higher "unnatural" rate which the monetarists have labeled "natural" because it sounds better than the reality which is "high unemployment". But common sense will allow us to have our cake and eat it too. To achieve price stability, however, we must achieve stable labor unit costs. And that is not practical in a full employment environment in the absence of an effective incomes policy to prevent the abuse of market power.

There is so much at stake. Consider a riddle. What do the provision of jobs for people who want to work, affordable housing for people who need homes, reduced carrying charges on the national debt, cheaper electricity, relief for farmers and a break for the Third World have in common? The answer? Lower interest rates! Why are current interest rates both so much more erratic and so much higher than they were 25 years ago? It is primarily due to inflation and the fear of inflation in conjunction with the deliberate policy of the Fed to use interest rates as its principal tool in damping wage-push inflation. There has to be, and is, a better way of wrestling inflation to the ground, and the high level of unsustainable interest rates with it.

INCENTIVE INDEXING

Incentive indexing is the most appropriate way to

describe my proposed incomes policy with its limited but essential objective. It is not to be mistaken for any system of comprehensive wage and price controls because it is not comparable. It is simply an antidote to the special immunities already granted to labor unions and a complement to antitrust and anticombines laws that are quite impotent to cope with the peculiar characteristics of oligopolistic industry. It prescribes rules designed to prevent the abuse of power while at the same time encouraging both business and labor to enjoy the benefits of increased efficiency and the resulting higher real incomes.

There is little point in submitting to a disastrous recession and then sitting idly by and watching the inflationary spiral begin afresh a few months later. As the Fed tacitly admits when it raises interest rates, the market power of big business and big unions, which gave rise to the problem, will not have disappeared in the interim. Consequently, some kind of incomes policy is necessary to act as a permanent "temperature control" to keep wages and prices from exploding.

Unfortunately, the record of success of incomes policies to date is not a happy one; thus many experts dismiss the idea except for use in emergencies. Still there are economists who seem to share my conviction that past failures are attributable to a combination of careless design and inconsistent application rather than to the concept itself. Arthur Burns, former Chairman of the Board of Governors of the Federal Reserve System, with whom I discussed the problem on more than one occasion, once told me that governments will continue to experiment with incomes policies. He said they will apply them, then take them off again; try again and then backtrack, until somebody, somewhere, eventually gets it right.

There have been a variety of experiments to date and while some were quite successful for extended periods they eventually failed for predictable reasons. Many were voluntary and consequently were doomed from the outset. Others had bureaucrats establishing wages and prices – a system which has never worked except briefly during an emergency such as wartime. Still others distributed the benefits of technology on the basis of specific industries which was both unfair and seen to be unfair.   Inevitably the practice led to failure and abandonment.

In the United States, the *Annual Report of the President's Council of Economic Advisers* set out criteria for both unions and management in 1962.   The concept received general support for a few years, when it enjoyed a protective umbrella of civic responsibility.   But by 1966 public discipline had pretty well evaporated, and whether the breakdown resulted from the Vietnam War or simply bigger wage demands is, in a sense, irrelevant.   The lid on prices was effectively blown.

In August 1971 President Nixon confounded the experts by reversing his policy and introducing compulsory controls. Prices, incomes and dividends were frozen for ninety days while spot checks were undertaken to ensure compliance.   Phase Two was a period of tight controls following the freeze.   Price stability during this period was encouraging – so much so, in fact, that Mr. Nixon moved on to Phase Three, which meant a return to voluntary controls.   It didn't take long thereafter for conditions to return to "normal", with the whole plan being abandoned.

President Carter's October 1978 initiative launched "a program of price and pay standards designed to brake the price-wage spiral that has beset our economy for more than a decade."[1] His voluntary program included an explicit numerical ceiling for wage and fringe benefits, as well as a price deceleration standard for individual firms.

In January 1979 the President's Council underlined the difficulty with voluntary plans: "One of the obstacles to the success of voluntary wage and price standards is fear on the part of each group of workers that their observance of the wage standard could lead to a loss of real income if others do not cooperate, or if uncontrollable events, such as a serious crop shortage, result in price increases.   Faced with such uncertainty and basing their price expectations on recent patterns of inflation, any workers might be reluctant to cooperate with the standards program.   To improve the acceptability of the standards, the Administration is proposing to the Congress an innovative program of real wage insurance for those who observe them."[2]

Unfortunately, Congress did not pass the real wage insurance law as requested by the President. Furthermore, the courts rejected the legality of a system that lacked legislative authority.[3] So the guidelines remained voluntary in the literal sense.

"Studies by the Council of Economic Advisers reinforce the view that the President's program aided in keeping wage rates from accelerating.... However, both the employment cost index for union workers, and the effective wage change in collective bargaining units covering 1,000 workers or more, showed a greater increase in the 4 quarters through September 1979 than in the preceding 4 quarters."[4] At the same time productivity decreased and labor unit costs jumped by 11.3 percent, compared with 7 or 8 percent over the same four quarters a year earlier.[5]

No lesson from past experience could be clearer than the observation that voluntary systems are essentially useless except for very brief periods at a time of acknowledged national crisis.   To reinforce this conclusion, I have often asked audiences what their attitude would be if income tax was voluntary. Would they pay more, the same, or less tax than now required by law? Usually a couple of altruists insist that they would pay the same; but the overwhelming majority admit honestly that they would remit considerably less if the amount were open to their discretion.

The principle is straightforward. Most people will obey laws that appear to be just if they are fairly enforced. But they will also take advantage of any concessions, opportunities, privileges, or even loopholes permitted by the law. In the words of that great nineteenth-century liberal John Stuart Mill, "the interference of law is required, not to overrule the judgement of individuals but to give effect to that judgement: they being unable to give effect to it except by concert, which concert again cannot be effectual unless it receives validity and sanction from the law."[6]

GUIDELINES NOT REQUIRED IN THE MARKET SECTOR

If an incomes policy must be mandatory to be effective, the next question that arises is whether or not it should apply to the whole economy. And, if not, what segments should be exempt? The day that President Nixon's wage and price freeze was invoked in August 1971, I predicted that the controls would ultimately fail because they were attempting the impossible – never a sound foundation for economic policy. My objection was based on two factors: first, the inclusion of commodities, especially food; second, the simplistic treatment of the economy as one animal, without regard to the dichotomy between the market and oligopolistic sectors.[7]

Because I was raised on a farm, and one of my first business ventures was marketing fruit, I was particularly sensitive on the first point. I recalled how quickly prices changed in response to supply and demand. Strawberries were an extreme case. A price set early in the season, when the berries first appeared, would be unrealistically high a week later. Similarly, a price set in mid-season would be far too low in early or late season, when supplies were scarce. The same problem applied to a lesser extent with other foods and many internationally traded commodities. While it is easy to pass regulations attempting to control prices in these cases, it is not easy to enforce them when they don't make sense in light of market conditions.

Just as it is impossible to effectively control the prices of commodities, which fluctuate with changing supply and demand, it is not necessary to impose controls where genuine market conditions exist. If it is theoretically possible for monetary policy to regulate prices in a free market economy, then it should be possible to regulate that part of the economy which is genuinely "free". One does not need to interfere with the market where the market actually governs.

The problem, as I explained earlier, is not the market. It is the fact that the "free" or market sector is frustrated in its operation by wage and price leadership from the sector that is, by definition, rigid. The economy is like two horses tied to the same wagon. The stronger horse – the one with market power – pulls out in front. So instead of a team, you have a lead horse getting out of line and tending to pull the wagon around in circles. A steady pull requires either an inflationary monetary policy, so that the laggard can keep up, or a tether on the lead horse.

The object of an essential incomes policy, then, is to control labor unit costs in the rigid sector and then to ensure that the benefits of increased productivity are shared by all members of society. Stated as a principle, the function of an incomes policy is to do the job that antitrust and anticombines laws were intended to do, have failed to do, and never can do. It is to keep the monopolies and oligopolies, the powerful lead horse, in harness with the rest of the economy so that the whole can move forward together.

There is bound to be some difference of opinion as to who should be subject to regulation and who should not. Generally speaking, guidelines should apply to all monopolies, oligopolies, and cartels - all cases of "less than perfect" market conditions. This view has been expressed by others, including J.K. Galbraith, who has long promoted the concept.[8]

There will always be borderline cases where it is not entirely clear whether an industry is oligopolistic or not, so it should be possible for each company or industry to opt either for the free or the controlled sector. When a company or industry opts in favor of the regulated sector, it should have the protection of the law with regard to prices. That means that it would be exempt from anticombines law in respect of pricing, and that the public interest would be protected by observance of the profit guidelines laid down in the incomes policy.

When, on the other hand, a company or industry chooses in favor of the free and uncontrolled sector it must, in fact, compete in respect to prices as well as in other areas. Should there be any evidence of price fixing, identical bidding, or lack of genuine competition at any time, the choice should be subject to appeal. The public interest must be given the benefit of the doubt.

Official recognition of the existence and legitimacy of oligopolies would not eliminate the necessity for public review of mergers and takeovers. But observance of guidelines set by an incomes policy should relieve officers and directors of companies from the threat of going to jail for doing what comes naturally.

On the labor side, all collective agreements should be assumed to be monopolistic in nature and subject to the policy. Of course there are cases where this is not literally true. Small unions have been broken and non-union labor hired. But for all practical purposes the big unions do constitute a monopoly labor supply. Trying to differentiate between the big unions that do constitute a monopoly and the little ones that might not is too difficult and conducive to acrimony. So there is no simpler test, nor one easier to administer; a collective agreement, by definition, must be subject to the policy.

WHO SETS PRICES AND WAGES?

One final question remains. If big business and organized labor should be subject to an incomes policy, who should set the individual prices and wages? Looking for the answer takes us back to earlier experiments, including wartime experience. Almost everyone who was then involved in controlling prices is against the reimposition of controls. But why? Controls did seem to work for some time under emergency conditions when there was widespread public support for them. But later, anomalies appeared that led to black markets and other arrangements of convenience.

As always, the original prices had been those previously set by the trade. But as costs went up, and profit margins were squeezed, there was no quick, effective way to cope. Even when it was permissible for extra costs to be "passed through", the bureaucratic machinery was too cumbersome to avoid unacceptable delays. So businesses adopted survival tactics of cutting quality, taking under-the-table payments, or removing the product from the market altogether.

Even when control prices are set by "experts", the results are likely to be unsatisfactory. An example from my own experience in the housing business is illustrative. To encourage the production of houses to meet the desperate post-war shortage, the Canadian government had its agency, the Central (now Canada) Mortgage and Housing Corporation, insure high-ratio mortgage loans. For a builder to qualify, however, the CMHC retained the right to set the retail price of the house.

By the early 50's the market had eased to the point where, in many cases, the government's maximum price had become a convenient "minimum". Sellers confronted buyers with the fact that the asking price had been set by the government and in this way used the official figures to sustain prices higher than would have been set by the market. It was an inflexible system, however, so several builders consulted the responsible minister about removing the controls. Inevitably, the reply from CMHC was always highly negative; price-setting would continue.

A builder myself, I volunteered to produce my company's cost sheets, which showed profit margins ranging from minus $400 to plus $1,900 a unit on the basis of the controlled prices.[9] Obviously, there was no incentive to build the unprofitable models, so purchasers were restricted in their choice. The minister through whom the CMHC reported to parliament, Bob Winters, was impressed, and two weeks later the controls were removed. Within a month new house prices in Toronto had fallen an average of $400 each.

In all the experiments with price controls and incomes policies to date, there is no case where a bureaucratic machine has been able to set prices quickly enough and accurately enough to be acceptable. It is my opinion that a bureaucratic structure could never do so; its expertise is too limited and its data too stale. Governments simply should not get involved in the business of price-fixing. They should opt, instead, for mandatory profit guidelines, an alternative that eliminates the possibility of black-marketeering and of product substitution or restriction for the purpose of circumventing regulations.

Experience has shown the "order of magnitude" of the long-term return on capital associated with each industry. No single formula need apply. Guidelines could be devised that would accommodate the special requirements of different types of industries and conglomerates and still leave them the autonomy required for successful operation.

There would have to be a provision to allow profit-averaging over some reasonable period, say four years. It would be unfair, as well as unworkable, to require compliance in each calendar or fiscal year. Industry is faced with too many variables to alter course abruptly, and needs the flexibility to permit long-range planning.

Sensible guidelines would have no effect on investment. New, entrepreneurial companies would be exempt because they are invariably competitive. Guidelines would only apply to mature, oligopolistic industry, and in more than 95 percent of cases the allowable profit would be well in excess of anything companies have been able to achieve in recent years.

I have avoided specific figures because the purpose of this book is to discuss principles without getting bogged down in controversy over whether a specific industry should be allowed a 15 or 20 percent return on invested capital. But in all cases the guidelines would be more than adequate to maintain investor interest.

For the same reasons that government is not qualified to set individual prices, it should avoid getting involved in setting individual wages. The bureaucratic machinery required would bog down hopelessly. Not only that, it would just be a duplication of the existing facilities available to management and labor. So government should limit itself to the determination of an over-all wage guideline based on the previous year's increase in real output per member of the labor force adjusted to reflect any redistribution of income, either domestic or external, that might have to be taken into account.

Once the figure has been set, adjustments to individual wages and salaries should be made through direct management-labor channels. The only overriding criterion must be that the total package, including fringe benefits and wage drift[10] – a

general job reclassification that results in higher average pay
– does not exceed the limit set by the policy.   This doesn't
mean that no one would ever get an increase greater than the
guideline.   Privates would still be promoted to corporal, and
corporals to sergeant.   Assistant general managers would
become general managers and earn the raise consistent with
their increased responsibilities.   This is all provided for in the
system.   Only an attempt to accelerate the tempo of promotion
for the sole purpose of cheating on the guidelines would destroy
their effect and consequently would be prohibited.

AVERAGE WAGE INCREASES MUST EQUAL AVERAGE PRODUCTIVITY GAINS

The reason the wage guideline must be based on the
average increase in real output is because there is such a vast
range of productivity rates between earth-moving, petro-
chemicals and manufacturing, for example, on the high end of
the scale, and some of the service industries like education and
health care on the low end.   In these cases productivity, as we
measure it, may be zero or even negative when more doctors
and nurses are required for a complicated operation or when
the number of students per teacher is reduced in order to
provide more time with each.

It would be unjust and unworkable, to give workers in
high productivity industries big increases and those in many
service industries no increase at all.   Indeed, in jurisdictions
where this has been tried the system has failed miserably.
Taking an average is the only way that both justice and price
stability can be achieved.   The cost of some services, where the
guideline exceeds productivity increases, will rise.   The cost
(price) of most manufactures, where wage increases are less
than productivity increases, must come down.   Lower prices
for manufactured products will offset higher prices for services
and in this way price stability will be achieved.

PROFIT SHARING

Although union wages would be indexed to average productivity increases, and this tractor-trailer relationship should
be sufficient incentive for everyone to pull together to increase
output, a powerful case can be made for allowing profit-sharing
agreements as an added bonus. I personally would both permit
and encourage collective agreements providing for a bonus to
workers of some modest percentage of a company's pre-tax
profits – through either direct or deferred profit-sharing plans.

This idea was promoted by the late Walter Reuther when
he was President of the United Auto Workers. It was not
popular with management at the time, but as the years pass it
is being recognized as the type of concession whereby corporations have little to lose and much to gain. Executives award
themselves bonuses for producing results and there is no reason
why the principle shouldn't apply to everyone involved. There
is, after all, nothing like a work force with a direct incentive
to be productive.

Workers would gain on both fronts. First directly, as
their company prospered, and then through higher wages as
better individual results contributed to a higher national average
of increased efficiency. There would be a strong incentive to
establish joint management-labor productivity councils in each
bargaining unit because everyone would benefit from the results
of initiative and imagination. Improved performance in
thousands of individual bargaining units would soon add up to
a measurable increase in the national guidelines.

ARBITRATING GRIEVANCES

One other point involves the internal redistribution of
income referred to earlier. It is inevitable, whenever an
incomes policy is applied, that some group or class of workers
would be caught at a disadvantage. This cannot be avoided,
and the best that can be done is to establish a body to hear
grievances and arbitrate claims for catch-up. This task might
be assigned to a wage board appointed exclusively, or at least

predominantly, from the ranks of trade unions. The board would hear and evaluate complaints and decide how much catch-up, if any, was justified and the time frame over which it would be allowed.

All awards of this kind would have to fit within the total sum provided by law and excluded from general distribution. In other words, the general guideline would be a little bit less than the average increase in output for the previous year so that there would be a small pool available for the cases of catch-up – at least in the early years until the most blatant distortions had been ironed out.

ENFORCEMENT

Enforcement of all wage and profit guidelines would be effected by means of the income and corporations tax laws. A schedule of profit guidelines would be incorporated at the outset and amended only if experience proved that they were too restrictive. The wages guideline would be amended each year to reflect the average productivity increase for the previous year and while it would not apply to non-union labor it would give employers a clear indication of what would be inflationary and what would not.

Using the existing tax laws is the simplest and most efficient method of enforcement because the Internal Revenue System in the United States and Revenue Canada in Canada are well equipped for the task and no expensive new bureaucracy is required. Excess wage and profit increases would simply be taxed at 100 percent, with additional penalties for cases of deliberate non-compliance.

This is not the place to set out the specifics of an incomes policy. The staff work involved should be undertaken in partnership by government, management, and labor. Not only is any system more likely to be acceptable if it is developed in a spirit of cooperation, but early private sector involvement should guarantee the avoidance of many pitfalls.

Even then, some minor flaws are to be expected. The late Arthur Burns would likely have agreed that the probability of developing a "perfect system" is too remote to be taken seriously. Like Marx's long-awaited withering away of the state, the notion of an earthly Utopia will remain a will-o'-the-wisp as long as there are people involved. The most we can hope for is a system that avoids some of the grievous errors associated with previous experiments and embodies principles compatible with the real economic environment in which it would be applied.

THE TIP: AN ALTERNATIVE?

I have tried to incorporate all the significant lessons from past experience into the design of a better system. Still, I am sure someone will wonder if I have considered the merits of alternative ideas such as the concept of a tax-based incomes policy (TIP) as proposed by Wallach & Weintraub and endorsed by the *New York Times* in a lead editorial in 1983.[11]

A tax-based incomes policy is one that can either reward workers for limiting pay increases to a prescribed level or penalize them if they don't. Similarly companies could be rewarded for limiting price increases to an established guideline or penalized for non-compliance. It is very different from my formula in its breadth of application and the complexity of operation.

The 1981 *Annual Report of the President's Council of Economic Advisers* discusses tax-based incomes policies at some length: "Several choices must be made in designing a TIP. First, should it dispense rewards or levy penalties? Second, should receiving the penalty or reward depend only on being above or below the standard (a 'hurdle ' TIP), or should the size of the penalty or reward be graduated in accordance with the difference between the standard and the actual pay or price increase (a 'continuous' TIP)? Third, should the TIP apply to pay, to prices, or to both? These choices require striking a balance among equity, efficiency, administrative ease and effectiveness in reducing inflation."[12]

The Council concludes: "For several reasons, a reward pay TIP is probably preferable to a penalty pay TIP." This would cost a substantial amount in forgone revenues (tax credits), however, so "a reward TIP would only be feasible when tax cuts were being considered.... A TIP limited to a few thousand large firms with computerized personnel records would have much smaller public and private administrative costs than a TIP that included millions of small firms." But this "would be vigorously opposed by workers in small firms, who would argue, rightly, that they were being deprived of a potential tax cut."[13]

The final major issue, the Council suggests, is whether a TIP should be permanent or temporary. "The answer seems to be that a permanent TIP would not be feasible because of the distortions it would create by discouraging changes in relative wages. A TIP might introduce further distortions as people changed their behavior to circumvent the intent of the policy while remaining technically in compliance with the standard."[14]

"On balance", concluded the Council, "a temporary hurdle TIP - a tax credit to groups of workers whose average pay increase does not exceed a specified standard – seems superior to other variants." This would probably have to be coupled with a price TIP for political reasons "because restraints on pay alone, even with a reward TIP, might appear inequitable." The Council estimated that for a cost of $12 billion its temporary, voluntary system might reduce wage inflation by .79 to .93 percent, depending on the pay standard set. For $16 billion, an improvement of .91 to 1.09 percent might be expected.[15]

To impose such a complicated system for such a small benefit seems to me a little bit ridiculous. The plan fails to recognize either the permanent nature of the power and influence of monopolies and oligopolies or the likelihood that the wage-price spiral would resume its upward trend when the TIP was abandoned. A TIP, in my opinion, would be just another temporary expedient, which, like President Carter's voluntary scheme, might be better than nothing, but not much better.

It is axiomatic that stable prices are impossible without constant labor unit costs. Therefore it follows that inflation will exit permanently only with an incentive-indexed incomes policy that deals forcibly and realistically with the structural effects of monopoly power. To do this it must (a) be mandatory, (b) be permanent, (c) apply only to the rigid sector of the economy, and (d) allow companies and their unions to set their own prices and wages within the parameters set down by the policy.

ACHIEVING A CONSENSUS

Often when I speak on this subject people will say: "It sounds good, but you will never get big business and big labor to agree." Without underestimating the extent of the selling job to be done, I respectfully disagree. I would never propose a policy that I believed to be beyond the realm of practical politics. In addition, I have delivered literally hundreds of lectures on the subject and the acceptance rate of the audiences – people who say "Why don't we try it?" – has always been between 60% and 70%, and there has been little difference between union and non-union audiences. The same level of support has been registered in radio and television polls.

I will never forget one particular experience when I was giving my spiel on television. Half-way through the program I suddenly realized that the cameramen were all union members and I was concerned as to what they might be thinking. I decided to play it cool and kept going. At the end of the program all three came up to chat and to assure me that what I had been saying, in their opinion, made a lot of sense. One of them even said: "Mr. Hellyer, I would buy a used car from you" which I considered one of the better compliments of my political career.

This experience simply confirmed that the average person is no fool and if you give people the facts the majority will be persuaded, because the arithmetic is simple. For 27 years U.S. workers produced 0.8% more goods and services, on average, than they did the year before (see Table 1, page 131). If that trend were to continue everyone could have an annual wage increase of 0.8% without increasing labor unit costs and subsequently prices. Should anyone get more than

that it would be either at someone else's expense (a redistribution of income) or, if the Fed permitted an increase in the
money stock to accommodate the bigger wage gains, a contribution to inflation.

That is what happened for the 27 years from 1964-1991.
Wage increases averaged 6% which resulted in average inflation
of 5.2% - representing the difference between real output and
nominal wage gains initiated by monopoly power and made
possible by increases in the money stock. The illusive gains
were of no benefit to labor, however, because Figure 14
demonstrates very clearly that real wages are tied directly to
real output and bear no relationship to nominal wages.
Obviously workers have nothing to lose and much to gain from
accepting settlements based on real increases in output. In fact
that is the most likely way to increase overall productivity and
real wage gains.

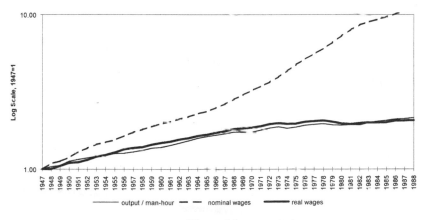

U.S. - Indexes of Productivity: Real and Nominal Compensation, Private Non-farm
Industries (1947-1988)

Figure 14

Source: U.S. Monthly Labor Review, 1989.

The second reason for acceptance is that for the country
as a whole there is no other choice. Interest rates must come
down. If they don't, even the strongest of nations, the United

States, will be brought to its economic knees.   Figure 15
illustrates how the debt burden will increase over time without
a dramatic change in policy.   The figures chosen for rates of
growth in GDP and debt are purely arbitrary, but the trend
isn't.   The trend is real!   The trend indicates that the United
States is headed for its biggest ever economic crisis.

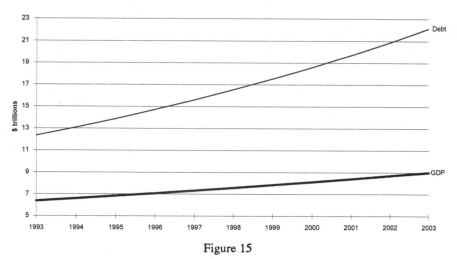

Figure 15

SIMULATIONS CONFIRM BENEFITS

The benefit of an incomes policy along the lines of the
one proposed was tested for the Canadian economy for the
years 1978-1985.   Two different simulations were run and,
despite very conservative assumptions, the benefits were
striking.   Inflation would have been held at a low level, there
would have been 870,000 additional jobs in 1985, and the debt
of governments (federal and provincial) would have been
reduced $50 billion to $82 billion depending on the assumptions
concerning appreciation of the Cdn. dollar versus the U.S.
dollar.   For technical reasons, the tests could not be extended
to 1992 but the economists involved estimated that had it been

possible the debts of governments would have been $220 billion less.[16] That would have avoided most of Canada's current economic problems.

In view of the fact that the U.S. economy is roughly ten times the size of Canada's it is not unreasonable to assume that had the U.S. adopted a common sense incomes policy prior to the 1981-82 recession instead of choosing monetarism the federal debt in 1994 would be $2 trillion less, at the very least.

SUMMARY

In spite of the facts, there will be business and union leaders who resist change. One top union official told me: "Of course you're right, but we'll fight you in the trenches." I have no doubt of that and I suspect that one of the most comic aspects of any campaign would be the sight of union leaders and bank presidents on the same platform defending "free enterprise" and "free collective bargaining" with all the intense sincerity that would be justified if access to banking and unions was really free and unrestricted. In the end their view would not and could not prevail, however, because it would be undermined by the good sense of the majority for whom they presumed to speak.

CHAPTER 11

OTHER THINGS

"I repeat ... that all power is a trust - that we are accountable for its exercise - that, from the people, and for the people, all springs and all must exist."

Benjamin Disraeli

If economists had designed some system of debt-free money-creation to parallel the unprecedented production of goods unleashed by the industrial revolution we might have avoided many, if not all, of the financial crises of the last two hundred years. More money was needed to buy all of that increased supply and the happenstance of gold was seldom synchronized with the potential of the real economy.

Admittedly it might have been difficult in the nineteenth century, complicated as it was by so many wars and the desire of the monarchs to impose future taxes through borrowing rather than expose to public view the real cost of their ambitions. But there is far less excuse for the twentieth century and one can only speculate as to how an effective, common-sense, monetary system might have changed the course of history. It is even possible that the second World War might have been avoided if we had not been subjected to that horrendous, monetary Great Depression which spawned dictatorships

160

of the left and right.   Most economists now admit that the depression could have been avoided but how unfortunate it is that their insight has been pretty well limited to hindsight.

TABLE 2

Rates of Growth for Key Economic Indicators: 1948-1993 (in percent)

Economic Indicator	1948-1973	1974-1993

1. GNP or GDP
    * GNP in 1982 dollars
    ** GDP in 1987 dollars
	3.70*	2.28**

2. Per Capita Disposable Income
    * In 1982 dollars
    ** In 1987 dollars
	2.45*	1.32**

3. Average Hourly Earnings
    * In 1982 dollars
    ** In 1987 dollars
	2.19*	-0.73**

4. Average Weekly Earnings
    * In 1982 dollars
    ** In 1987 dollars
	1.84*	-1.06**

5. Median Family Income
    * In 1980-82 dollars
    ** 1974-1992 in 1987 dollars
	2.80*	0.14**

6. Output per Hour per Person
    * Non-farm business sector
    ** 1974-1992
	2.51*	0.83**

7. Output per Man Year
    * GNP per employed person in 1982 dollars
    ** GDP per employed person for 1974-1992
       in 1987 dollars
	1.72*	0.59*

8. Industrial Production	4.64	2.06
9. Manufacturing Production	6.07	2.45
10. Total Non-Agricultural Employment	1.17	1.82
11. Manufacturing Employment	1.00	-0.62
12. Services Employment	2.54	2.95
13. Government Employment* * Federal, state, and local	3.60	1.59
14. Federal Government Employment	1.32	0.45

Sources: Economic Report of the President, 1991, 1994

After the War there were some of us who actually believed that we had learned from past experience and that our economic future was assured. We had a judicious mix of government-created and bank-created money. Debt to GDP ratios first declined and then held steady, jobs were available for people who wanted to work, inflation was slight, productivity was high and incomes were rising.

Alas, the fifteen "golden years" passed all too soon. Wage settlements began to lose all relevance to productivity. Inflation began to rise. The proportion of government-created money began to fall. The "counter-revolution in monetary theory", as Prof. Friedman calls it, came on the world stage at precisely the wrong time. What other conclusion can you come to if you review the data and note the increase in money creation, debt, debt to GDP ratios and unemployment levels that correspond to the era of monetarism's predominance in mainline economics? Table 2 provides a stark comparison in U.S. economic performance before and after monetarism held sway.[1]

Monetarism's naive faith in the invisible hand of free market adjustments has already given the Western world two very serious disasters and is setting us up for an even greater one. Mainline economics is leading capitalism down the garden path toward the point where it will collapse of its own debt weight. So now is the time to take a hard look at all the factors. It is not too late to change course but time is running out. Far better to act now then to provide work for more future economists analyzing what went wrong and how the disaster could have been avoided.

To arrange a proper marriage between the financial and real economies will require greater adjustments than would have been necessary when they were younger and less set in their ways. Even a cursory look will show that there is no single step which will cure the chronic problems of inflation, high unemployment, high interest rates, large deficits and excessive debt. There are a number of interlocking steps that must be taken. From my perspective they fall into two classes – those that are essential and those that may be desirable or at least worth looking at. The three that I consider essential in order to have a fair shot at meeting all the principal objectives, are: (a) monetary reform, (b) an incomes policy (other than monetarism) and (c) tighter banking regulations.

1. <u>Monetary Reform</u>. The way money is created must
be changed so there is less reliance on debt. The objects and
benefits of moving gently but firmly away from near-total
reliance on a fractional reserve banking system are many and
profound. It will be easier for federal governments to achieve
and maintain balanced budgets and, with the increased facility
available to them, to share burdens with other levels of government so that state and city governments, too, will be able to
balance revenue and income. In addition, the change will, over
time, substantially increase bank reserves as a proportion of
liabilities. This will make them less vulnerable to "runs" and
failures from any cause. It will make the world system less
volatile and subject to collapse. An extra dividend is that the
public's contingent liability for deposit insurance will be
substantially reduced as banks begin to operate more like the
kind of business they would lend to if they were lending to
themselves. This will reduce the banks' dependence on governments to print "funny money" (legal tender) to bail them out
and keep them solvent in times of emergency.

The importance of giving governments greater latitude,
without the necessity of raising the entire sum by means of
higher explicit taxes, is a function of changes in life style and
priority. As America has moved from a family-oriented,
agriculture-dominated to a more industrialized, impersonal
society, many of the functions formerly financed by the family
must now be financed by the state. In a predominantly
agricultural America families cared for the sick and the elderly
at home. While there is much nostalgia for that system it is not
possible, in the majority of circumstances, to turn the clock
back. This is especially so in families that require two incomes
in order to pay for the basic necessities.

In addition, industrialization creates new and increased
responsibility for the state. Private enterprise invents, develops,
manufactures and profits from the sale of automobiles. The
state is then obliged to build and maintain roads and bridges.
Private enterprise invents, develops, manufactures and profits
from the sale of airplanes. The state is required to build and
maintain airports and provide customs and immigration services

as people in larger numbers travel out of country. The list could go on and on but the bottom line is that governments spend a much larger share of total national income than they did until recent decades and if the whole is raised by explicit taxes the level of taxation becomes a disincentive. New taxes may also contribute to cost (tax)-push inflation.

2. An Incomes Policy. This is absolutely essential to maximize the benefit from monetary reform. If the new money created each year is distributed vertically, through higher wages for the already employed and consequently higher prices for existing output, it will neither be available to finance additional employment nor increase output. If there is any one concept which must be learned in order to understand the failure of monetarism it is this. To the extent that the increase in money stock – translated into income – is distributed vertically, in excess of increases in productivity, it contributes to higher wages and prices rather than increased output. Unless wage increases to the already employed are limited to the average increase in real output, inflation will continue and if inflation continues interest rates will be higher than necessary because lenders will continue to demand a premium as a hedge against the anticipated inflation. This has negative implications for governments and for the economy as a whole. It is the people who must bear the extra burden. Continued inflation would also encourage economists to trot out the Phillips Curve as an excuse for the higher unemployment levels that they claim are "natural". If there is one benefit which tops the list from a humanitarian point of view it is the availability of jobs for people who want to work. This has been the over-riding motive in my life-long obsession with economics because I think the need to contribute to the common well-being is fundamental to one's feeling of self worth. Finally, it should be noted, negligible inflation protects the value of savings for everyone.

3. Tighter Banking Regulations. The thought of regulations gives bankers nightmares. The only regulations they really like are the ones they develop themselves like reducing reserve requirements from the original 50% at the time the Bank of England was first chartered to as low as 3% or even

0% for certain kinds of deposits today. If they are to continue to have any special privilege to "print" money, even if it is only half as much as they have previously enjoyed, banks will have to review and rework the whole concept of the "public trust" that this implies.

Nothing irritates me quite as fast as a bank spokesperson saying, in response to the suggestion that they make more money available to small business, "We have to act as guardians of our depositors' money." Such fatuous double-speak! What they are really saying is that we, and we alone, will decide for whom we will create loans and we prefer governments, brokers and big business because that way we can make more money for less work. If they were only concerned about the safety of existing deposits they would have been less cavalier in making loans to Third World governments, large real estate developers and the leveraged-buyout monopoly players. It was the banks' greed, rather than their prudence as guardians of their depositors' money, which ruled the day.

If the whole idea of creating new money is to facilitate the creation of new wealth in the form of increased output, then the entire addition to the money stock should be directed to that purpose.   In effect new loans should be made for either investment or consumption because they are the two sides of the same coin! I cannot remember a market for anything that some enterprising entrepreneur didn't try to capitalize on. But if, as in the Great Depression and in one or two recent recessions, existing capacity exceeds demand, entrepreneurs are unlikely to line up for loans to create additional redundant capacity. So consumption, which creates income and savings for others, and investment are Siamese twins which cannot be separated.

It is the small businesses, which create the most jobs and increased output, that have the most difficulty getting bank financing. In the Spring of 1994, Helen Sinclair, president of the Canadian Bankers Association, cited one of the best known excuses. She admitted that banks have a problem in their relationship with small business but defended their caution by pointing out that federal government statistics show 50 percent of all small businesses don't make it past their fifth birthday.[2] That may be so but an equally interesting and important statistic would be the percentage which failed because their bank took away the safety net just as they jumped from the high wire. As I mentioned earlier, I have never known an entrepreneur, myself included, whose bank didn't try to put them out of business at one stage or another of their development. It would be in the country's interest if a certain proportion of new loans had to be made to small business with limited or no collateral where the investors, as a condition, were willing to risk their own savings. Character assessment might be part of the consideration. It is one which appears to have been pretty well disregarded in recent decades. Having considered that, the banks should be prepared to lose and write off some proportion of the small loans each year. It should satisfy their irresistible urge to gamble if they were to gamble on people who want to build real products and provide real services for a change.

This brings me to what banks should increasingly not be allowed to do. They should not be allowed to create money to make loans to foreign governments. Instead they might pool a little money and provide microbanking facilities to the world's potential entrepreneurs capable of providing employment and income to the teeming millions struggling to escape their poverty. It probably won't win me any marks to quote Chairman Mao but he spoke wisely when he said "Give a man a fish and you feed him for a day; teach a man to fish and you feed him for a lifetime." If the American dream means anything, it is a sign of wisdom to extend that dream to the widest extent possible both at home and worldwide.

One other banking practice that should be phased out as rapidly as possible is making loans for the purchase of stocks and bonds on margin. Buying stocks on margin is a classic example of spreading new money vertically to increase the price of the stocks without increasing the underlying real value of the assets. It is classic inflation. If stock ownership is supposed to represent savings, let it represent real savings instead of leverage.

Nowhere is the prohibition more urgent than in respect to companies buying shares in other companies with borrowed money and then deducting the interest from income for tax purposes. This particular raid on the treasury is as direct and rewarding as an armed hold-up. The only difference is that one is legal and the other is not. It is a practice, however, which should be ended because it creates no new wealth and adds to the concentration of existing wealth at taxpayers' expense. The chief financial officer of a large Canadian conglomerate once said that it was his job to see that no one company under his umbrella paid tax in any one year. The high leverage operation he was associated with did suffer some pain when the 1990-91 recession struck but meanwhile the government facilitated transfer of wealth from the poor to the rich owners of the conglomerate was staggering.

There are two important exceptions to this rule that I would recommend to policy makers reflecting on the question. The first would be some figure – say $50,000 credit – as a loan limit to all citizens equally for the purchase of shares. The purpose is two-fold. Although the number of applicants might not be great at first, use of the facility would extend the benefits of capitalism to a greater number of people and at the same time would allow employees to purchase shares in their company and participate as owners as well as workers. Employee Stock Ownership Plans (ESOPs) have been shown to be beneficial in that they produce a happier and consequently more productive work force. A Toronto Stock Exchange fact sheet reported: "Quantitative analysis also indicates that ESOP companies are dramatically outperforming their competitors in terms of profitability, return on equity, and return on capital. Further, these companies exhibit significantly lower debt-equity levels compared to other TSE-listed firms in their sectors."[3] The maximum figure chosen for the plan would have to be determined fiscally, i.e. how much income tax revenue could government afford to give up as a result of permitting the deduction of interest on the bank loans.

The second exception would be a much larger exemption for entrepreneurs buying shares in their own company in which they are engaged full time. This carrot would be a combination incentive and reward for the creation of new jobs and new wealth. It is an aspect of the American dream which should be encouraged. At the same time it is not a benefit which should apply equally to managers and officers of widely held companies. They have shown an amazing ingenuity in looking after their own interests so any stock they buy, in excess of the rule for all citizens, should be from after tax dollars, i.e. real savings.

Speculation in bonds and derivatives is even more worrisome. An article in the *New Federalist* sounds warning bells.

"Since the beginning of February, significantly more than $1 trillion worth of so-called 'financial assets' has been wiped out, in panic selling of leveraged positions built up using derivative instruments over the past five years of Federal Reserve-engineered declining interest rates. Down the tubes have gone the now-notorious 'hedge funds,' set up to circumvent the provisions of the Investment Company Act of 1940, and deploying an estimated 15-fold leverage on assets or collateral of up to $100 billion. Gone is J.P. Morgan's market in so-called 'emerging market debt.' Going, the so-called 'collateralized mortgage obligations' and their principal and interest 'strips'; going, the municipal bonds, as 'lenders' who have financed leveraged positions sell off the collateral in what is being described as 'a kind of global margin call.'

"And it's only the beginning. The trillion dollars-plus that evaporated over the last two months is embedded in the $12-16 trillion total notional value of global derivative instruments traded. That comes next.

"For example, U.S. banks have lent some 3.7% of their assets to finance margin purchases of bonds and other securities by borrowers like 'hedge funds.' That is more than $700 billion of such loans. And it is also some 2.5 times the paid-in capital of the banks. It doesn't include banks' purchases of securities for their own accounts. What they have lent has been put into hock by the borrowers to build up their leverage. Keeping such an inverted pyramid balanced on its apex is what the derivatives managers call 'risk management.'"[4]

Breaking the wild horses on this one will not be easy. Two approaches have been suggested. The first is to subject banks to fairly strict regulations as to the derivatives they can write. Congressman Henry B. Gonzalez, Chairman of the House Committee on Banking Reform and Urban Affairs has been leading the way on this front. The alternative is to impose a 0.1% tax on them as proposed by Lyndon LaRouche. In a March 28, 1993, press conference, Representative Gonzalez told those who were listening that adoption of such a tax would bring what has developed to a halt "overnight."[5]

There are several reasons why effective action of some kind is urgently required. The first, and probably most important, is to wean bankers away from the gambling mentality in favor of a development mentality. This is a big switch which will not happen easily or overnight. The second reason is that derivatives can be a major source of world market instability. No one I have talked to could say precisely the extent of the instability but the opinions ranged from significant to potentially critical. A combination of billions of exposure in derivatives, in the same wolf pack as other billions of hot money chasing around the world in search of speculative "opportunities", is enough to destabilize any system and render it vulnerable to collapse. It is a risk that can be avoided. Finally there is the question of reporting and of keeping shareholders fully informed as to how many of their chips are riding on what numbers. These are all good reasons to apply a harness.

If the banks do not want to operate in a way that treats money-creation as a public trust then the only alternative would be for governments to create all the new money, allow banks to lend only the real money depositors chose to entrust to them, and let them charge the full cost of the banking services they provide to those persons willing to pay. Personally I prefer the 50% solution proposed earlier because it is both politically and operationally more acceptable. But only if the banks are willing to accept a more limited and responsible role.

The principal points listed above are all essential if the economy is going to operate at or near its potential on a consistent basis. Each component is important in its own right but, as in baking, the final product is less than satisfying if you leave out one of the essential ingredients. It is a recipe that will require a lot of education, however. Very few policy makers understand the monetary system so they will have to learn before they can make the necessary adjustments.

CHANGES THAT ARE OPTIONAL – OR AT LEAST WORTH THINKING ABOUT

CONSTITUTIONAL AMENDMENTS

I am not one to recommend constitutional amendments but if there were extreme nervousness about government reclaiming its right to create part or all of the increase in the money stock, objectors might be placated by a constitutional safeguard to the effect that the increase in any one year could, under no circumstances, be more than proportional to the increase in real output for the preceding year, adjusted for the velocity of circulation and forecast changes in the size of the labor force. The provision could only be set aside by a seventy-five percent vote in both the Senate and the House of Representatives. The escape clause would never be used with the possible exception of a wartime emergency.

There is even less reason for a constitutional amendment requiring that the federal government budget be balanced. The idea is quite impractical without monetary reform. With monetary reform it is at least feasible. Given a boost from government-created money it should become the rule that all government budgets be balanced – with or without any constitutional rule to that effect.

MINIMUM WAGES

Few subjects are as controversial as to whether or not minimum wages are a good thing or a bad thing. As Linda Gorman points out in her essay on the subject in the *Encyclopedia of Economics*, "the minimum wage has had widespread political support enjoyed by few other public policies."[6]

She is quick to add, however, that "According to a 1978 article in *American Economic Review*, the American Economic Association's main journal, fully 90 percent of the economists surveyed agreed that the minimum wage increases unemployment among low-skilled workers. It also reduces the on-the-job training offered by employers and shrinks the number of positions offering fringe benefits. To those who lose their jobs, their training opportunities, or their fringe benefits as a result of the minimum wage, the law is simply one more example of good intentions producing hellish results."[7]

While I am well aware of these arguments, and of the potential consequences of minimum wages, I find a certain illogic in the objections. Economists say that minimum wages interfere with how wages are determined in a free market. But the market for labor is not free and the illogic arises in having a genuine market at the bottom end of the scale, for the poor, and a "wage leadership" driven monopoly at the top end. The result has been an increasing disparity between classes of workers. Figure 16 is indicative of the trend. The minimum wage was 46% of the average wage in manufacturing in 1959, and only 36% of that same index in 1993.

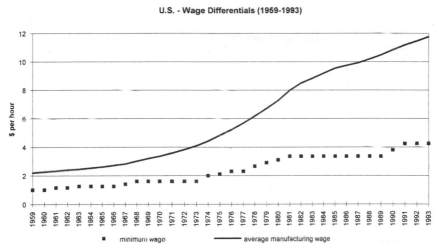

U.S. - Wage Differentials (1959-1993)

Figure 16
Source: Economic Report of the President, 1994, U.S. Department of Labor.

People working at or near minimum wages, who cannot afford to have faulty wiring or plumbing fixed or leaky roofs repaired, will be even worse off in the years ahead unless the trend is reversed. Either an incomes policy must narrow the gap between workers at the bottom of the heap and their more fortunate brothers and sisters, or else society must accept the consequences of a class system in which the majority earn more than enough to pay their own way, while the minority, comprising the "working poor", never will.

There has never been any doubt in my mind as to which route is preferable. It is really a matter of human dignity. Nobody should be forced to rely on subsidies and handouts. Yet if the incomes attached to some jobs are below the subsistence level, there is no other choice. Happily, the preferred solution is also the most economic, i.e. to raise settlements. By raising the bottom group a little more, and the top group a little less, the total will equal the total increase in output and there will be no inflationary effect.

Again, exceptions are in order. The object of the exercise is to increase the self-reliance of the working poor, and reduce their dependence on food stamps and subsidies which are a bureaucratically inefficient and costly way of redistributing income. So exemptions can be granted for three groups whose wages are not normally the only source of support. The groups are students, who have not yet become full-time members of the labor force, senior citizens past retirement age who usually have pension income plus personal savings as core income, and disabled or disadvantaged persons entitled to income at some level on that account. These three categories would provide a substantial market from which to fill marginal jobs at wages below the subsistence level.

TAXATION POLICY

Another area of at least academic interest is taxation policy. I know it is trendy and politically popular to have a graduated income tax system under which the rich pay higher marginal rates than the poor. I also realize that most of the rich and well-to-do people I know spend countless hours trying to determine how the high rates can be legitimately avoided. Their success, including helpful legislative changes, has been noteworthy.

I have often wondered if a flat-tax system couldn't be devised which would raise just as much income while at the same time, providing both an incentive to work hard and to pay tax. For discussion purposes it would be interesting to consider a flat-tax of, say, 20% on every dollar of income, including capital gains, over and above a standard non-taxable amount. Allow deductions of 50 percent of donations to charities and political parties, etc. up to the point where the rate was reduced to 15%, which would be the flat-tax minimum. I don't know how practical it would be but I am sure there is a system which would involve less income juggling and far fewer hours of accountants, and tax consultants, time.

If it were deemed expedient to collect a bit more from the rich, a tax on financial services would be one area to address. Collecting a tax on each purchase or sale of a security would be consistent with the concept of buying securities as investments rather than as chips in a poker game. Then there is that potentially lucrative tax on derivatives. The financial service industry would be less than enthusiastic but there is no good reason why it should be exempt from transaction taxes where some other industries are not so fortunate.

One kind of financial transaction which should be taxed is foreign exchange. This is an area which should be taxed, say at 1%, for each purchase or sale worldwide and the proceeds pooled to assist less-developed countries. Its purpose would be two-fold. First, to provide funds for Third World Development and, second, and of very great importance, to slow down the flow of hot money that circles the globe in search of vulnerable currencies. It is a prime source of instability and one that should be required to pay for its international mischief.

A WORLD DOLLAR
On the subject of currencies the time has come when it would be desirable to replace the U.S. dollar as a world

medium of exchange.   With the abandonment of the gold standard the void was filled by the British pound and the U.S. dollar. Over time the burden has fallen increasingly on the U.S. dollar with limited reliance on other currencies including the German mark and Japanese yen. The system works but it is a very great burden to fall so heavily on a single currency. The U.S. dollar should be free to rise and fall as a regulator of the U.S. balance of payments free of the responsibility for any possible impact on other world economies.

To succeed, a new world currency could not have a crazy name like ECU or Beaver. Perhaps World dollar would be most appropriate.   Whether the Bank for International Settlements (BIS) should have authority for its issuance I do not know. I am not a fan of the BIS, which has plotted the progressive deregulation of banks around the world, the drive for their independence from government and the new risk-based capital requirements as a substitute for cash reserves. In effect it has engineered a gigantic transfer of power from sovereign governments to autocratic banks. So I am skeptical of the BIS's credentials. But no matter where responsibility is assigned the new currency should be backed by all the world's currencies, as well as gold and silver, and the Bank should arrange swaps between currencies, and between currencies and metals, in order to facilitate trade as it evolves on a global scale.

Regardless of whether the BIS should be the issuer of a world currency, it definitely should not be the arbiter of reserve requirements for individual countries. These must be jealously guarded within national control. The currency of a country is the exclusive responsibility of sovereign governments and the ultimate responsibility for policy must not be delegated to either a national or international body. To do so is to negate and render obsolete the meaning of the word democracy.

Some of these ideas are presented for discussion purposes. There are many areas of reform that deserve a hard look. In the case of the three fundamentals, however, there is no option. Monetary reform, a common sense incomes policy and tighter banking regulations are the three pillars upon which a sane and stable economy can and must be built.

CHAPTER 12

A STAR TO STEER BY

"Like the spider, there are those of us who refuse to stop spinning, even when it would appear to be far more sophisticated to be without hope. Our rope, though perhaps frail, can still be spun with optimism, curiosity, wonder, love, and the sincere desire to share a trip to the stars. Our goal is worth the struggle, for in this case the star to which we aspire is full humanity for all."

Leo F. Buscaglia

Until a couple of years ago when people asked me to name the number one problem in Canada I would reply "the economy" without a moment's hesitation. Then I began to reflect on what I was saying and slowly but surely came to a different conclusion. The number one problem is the moral and spiritual breakdown of our society. The same conclusion would appear to be equally valid for the United States and the rest of the Western World which is floating in a sea of self-indulgence like a ship without a rudder.

That doesn't mean that our economies aren't in the pits, as I have tried to make perfectly clear in previous chapters. They are; but their condition is a symptom of the larger disease. They are what they are as a result of individual, collective and corporate greed and indifference towards the needs of others.

It is easy to blame politicians for the sad state of affairs but that is a classic example of passing the buck. Admittedly

there are few saints in the political world, and this scribe is
certainly no exception. But not everyone is willing to admit
that politicians' weaknesses and failures are a mirror of society.
In the summer of 1992, on a day when Canada's provincial
premiers were meeting in a last ditch effort to reach agreement
on constitutional amendments, a lady who lives in the same
condominium stopped me on the street and asked what I thought
the news was likely to be that night. In the course of the
discussion she launched into a diatribe against politicians which
concluded with the affirmation that they are all a bunch of
crooks. She only paused in mid-flight long enough to say –
when she suddenly remembered what I had been doing most
of my life – that in her opinion I was the sole exception. For
my part I felt obliged to remind her that politicians are, on
balance, a cross-section of the people who elect them.

There is no doubt in my mind that the ethical crisis is
not limited to the body politic. It extends to the population as
a whole. I was reminded of this when I took a close look at
a Federal Reserve note. I have no doubt that there was a time
when the Fathers of the Republic could honestly say "In God
we Trust"; but as an outside, though friendly, observer I
suspect that for the most part that time has long since gone.
Today it would appear more appropriate for the U.S. currency
to bear the inscription "In Power and Technology we Trust".
In saying that I am aware that the U.S. ranks splendidly as a
church-going nation. However, as is the case in my country,
a great part of that is habit and social custom. As a generator
of social change and as an example of moral rectitude the
roaring fire of the pilgrim fathers appears to have been reduced
to a few hot coals.

The United States can be rightfully proud of its achievement in space and landing the first man on the moon. If it had
spent one-tenth of one-percent as much scientific effort and
brainpower on the problems of unemployment and poverty, and
just a fraction of the cost of the space program in implementation, the ideas contained in this book would have been overtaken by time years ago. Instead we seem to be moving from
bad to worse. As Milton Friedman and Anna Jacobson

Schwartz point out in *A Monetary History of the United States 1867-1960*, the Fed could have taken action to mitigate the severity of the Great Depression of the 1930's which devastated the whole Western world.[1] Instead it took a devastating war to accomplish what our financial leaders were incapable of accomplishing. Following that dreadful war we enjoyed 20 years of prosperity – the longest stretch in the history of capitalism. The party could have lasted much longer had the most powerful members of society been content with fair shares. But that was not the case and when this excess was confronted by the monetarist theology it resulted in stagflation and then the two most disastrous recessions since the 1930's.

Each time the U.S. economy has slumped the consequences have been far-reaching. In 1930 the introduction of the Smoot-Hawley bill, with its protectionist stance, slowed the recovery process immeasurably.[2] Today the U.S. is a champion of free trade, but more in theory than in practice. In practice is uses U.S. law to frustrate free exchange and indulges in practices that range from tough to almost vicious. All of this in the name of protecting U.S. jobs and U.S. interests at a time when both of these are primarily the victim of U.S. domestic economic policy.

It seems to me, therefore, that any treatise on economics is incomplete without an attempt to put it in a philosophical context. We have already concluded that a privately-administered, decentralized system is the most productive. Individuals will work harder if they know that there will be rewards for their effort. Questions that remain include the means by which the maximum number of individuals will be allowed to participate, the limits between opportunity and exploitation, and the extent to which stewardship involves sharing with other members of the family of man.

It is especially fitting that 1994 should be both the UN International Year of the Family and the 50th Anniversary of D-Day, the invasion of Normandy by the most massive sea-launched military offensive in history. Allied veterans by the thousands returned on June 6th to those beaches which meant death to so many and hope to even greater numbers of those being liberated. So there were mixed emotions as they met for services of remembrance followed by dancing on the streets and reminiscing in the pubs.

It is easy to romanticize what the soldiers, sailors and airmen fought and died for. Perhaps some of them didn't even know. But most of the veterans who lived to express themselves say that they fought that men and women everywhere might be free – free to follow their own pursuits without fear, harassment or oppression. When pressed they admit that they did not risk their lives just to maintain the freedoms of speech, religion and expression; they thought it would be a world of justice, where people who wanted to work would be able to get jobs and where there would be freedom from poverty and homelessness.

The United Nations International Year of the Family is a timely reminder that our responsibilities extend beyond ourselves. A set of stamps beautifully designed by UN staff member Rocco J. Callari portrays the common themes against a common background of the International Year of the Family emblem – a heart sheltered by a roof and linked to another heart. The common background design is meant to symbolize life and love within a home. Each stamp has a different superimposed theme including the concept of inter-generational equality, responsible fatherhood, poverty in families, the value of the extended family, regional and international action on behalf of families and partnership in domestic responsibilities – struggles that are as ongoing as time itself.

Man has always looked for meaning in life beyond our day-to-day struggles for existence. It is not by accident that most North Americans admit at least token allegiance to one of the great religions of the world. What is more surprising is the extent to which there are common threads when it comes to questions such as sharing and responsibility for those members of society that are less well off than ourselves.

Both the Protestant and Catholic branches of the Christian church profess deep concern for the poor, the incapacitated and the disadvantaged. The great Archbishop of Canterbury, William Temple (1881-1944), once said that the church of Jesus Christ is the only cooperative society that exists for the benefit of its non-members.

This is in contrast to "the view that would limit the Church's action today, as always, to what is 'spiritual', and contends that it must, as far as possible, keep itself from involvement and contamination in the affairs of 'the world.'" "This", as a commission of the Church of Scotland goes on to say, "is quite unrealistic, comes near to being a form of religious escapism, and is based on a quite unscriptural idea of spirituality. It is, besides, false to the authentic record of the ministry and teaching of Christ, who spent a considerable part of His time healing men's bodies and made clear, in some of His parables and in His picture of the Last Judgment, that the final testing of men is in a very real way bound up with what they have done in the world to feed the hungry, clothe the naked, befriend the stranger, visit the sick and the prisoner. There is not a page of the New Testament but makes clear that practical ways of loving one's neighbour are an integral part of faith in God."[3] "He that loveth not his brother whom he hath seen, how can he love God whom he hath not seen."[4]

Robert J. Keller, O.P., whose doctoral dissertation is on Roman Catholic theology, says: "At the heart of a Catholic theological and philosophical understanding of the economy is the human person as agent, and more specifically, as worker. Humans bear the image of God, the Creator, therefore, we share in the imaginative activity of creating a world out of our labors.

"The source of economy is productive work. The Catholic tradition has long held that property, the product of work, belongs to its creator: the worker. This ownership, whether individual or collective, is never absolute; only God possesses the world. All property, goods, and ownership are measured by the welfare of the common good. Thus, economy is evaluated by what it does for people, to people, and how each one participates in it. At the very least, work is the means whereby persons provide basic sustenance for themselves and their families. Economic structures which explicitly or implicitly stifle this familial duty are unjust."[5]

The Reverend Friar continues: "Solidarity is a social virtue derived from the gospel demand to love each and all. When the demands of love appeal to justice for the most vulnerable and disadvantaged, the Church's social teaching speaks of an 'option for the poor.' In short, economy is a playing field of Christian love and justice, and the workaday world is the complement of the work of worship: liturgy."[6]

When I asked my good friend Rabbi David Monson, Rabbi Emeritus of Beth Sholom Synagogue, in Toronto, concerning Judaism's position in these matters he referred me to excerpts from Charity in Judaism. I must admit some surprise when I found that: "There is no word in the Hebrew language that really expresses the term 'Charity' as we know it. The Hebrew word that we use, Tzedaka, really means 'righteousness' and not 'Charity'.

"Why is this so?

"Simply because in Judaism there is a beautiful attitude toward the whole problem of giving alms to the poor. When you give to a needy person, you are doing only what is expected of you. You are doing the right thing. Judaism teaches us that it is a 'Mitzvah – *commandment*' to give aid where it is needed. It is not a matter of personal choice with us. On the contrary, we are obliged to share with those who are less fortunate than we. That is why the Hebrew language has no literal word for Charity. Whether we are rich or poor, great or small, high or lowly, we owe our fellow men help and sympathy, love and kindness. We have no right to decline any call for aid. We *must* help. We are unrighteous if we do not give aid. That is why the Hebrew word is Tzedaka – Righteousness."[7]

Although the Qur'an does not talk about love in the way that both the Jewish Bible and the New Testament do, its implied consequences of community and caring are fundamental to Islamic law. According to Jane I. Smith, Vice President and Dean of Academic Affairs, Iliff School of Theology, "The notion of responsibility to others is essential in Islam. It pervades the Qur'an, suggesting that one has the responsibility to care for the poor, for women, for widows and orphans, for strangers, and for any other people with needs. One of the five major responsibilities incumbent upon all Muslims is paying the almstax (zakat), which is roughly equivalent to a tithe. The reason for this is so that those who are needy can be taken care of. Sacrifice of animals at the major festival times is so that the meat of the animal sacrificed can be shared with the poor. There are many examples of this kind of concern. And it is clear that when one is judged at the day of the resurrection one of the elements of that judgment will be the basis of the degree to which one carried out one's responsibility to others in the community...

"Muslims believe that God is just, and because that is so humans are called upon to act justly to their fellows. In that way they not only carry out a human responsibility designated by God, but by acting justly actually acknowledge justice as a quality of the divine."[8]

"The fundamental principle of Buddhist ethics is that all men should develop an attitude of compassion – a very highly esteemed virtue in Buddhism. True wisdom consists not in metaphysical sophistication but in practical knowledge expressed in compassion as the fundamental principle in social life. Compassion or love in Sanskrit is *maitrī* (Pāli *mettā*), derived from *mitra* (friend). Thus, the term embodies the meaning 'true friendliness'. If one allows the virtue of compassion or love to grow in him, it will not occur to him to harm anyone else any more than he would willingly harm himself. By widening the boundaries of what one regards as his own, he breaks down the barriers that separate him from others."[9]

The ethical values of North American Aboriginal peoples include a sense of community, responsibility for other members of the tribe and a deep attachment to the earth which is considered almost holy.   "Morals set the limits and boundaries of personal behavior and ethics teach social behavior or the way individuals order their behavior with one another... By understanding ecological relationships and taking care to maintain them and learn from them, human beings maintain their own lives. We have also seen that North American sacred oral traditions teach people that they are dependent on each other and on many predictable and unpredictable things in the world.

"In Native communities, the moral and ethical behavior that was taught was really behavior that was necessary for survival in the natural world. The individual was taught to be responsible for his or herself but not in isolation from the rest of the community."[10]

When the basic philosophies of the vast majority of North Americans include belief in the dignity of work, the need for justice, the exercise of compassion and concern for ones neighbors you have to wonder how we managed to get our work-day practices so screwed up. Is there any justice in the fact that millions of people are unemployed involuntarily – and quite unnecessarily? Is it morally acceptable for people with monopoly power to use it in a way that contributes to the high level of unemployment? Is it right that some of the highest paid and most secure members of society should deliberately cause recessions that hurt and humiliate millions of the poorer and weaker members of society? And what is the moral judgment of economic policies that reduce the creation of wealth by trillions of dollars when there are needy outstretched hands from one corner of the globe to the other?

When I was writing about this subject in 1990 I was informed that one of every four children born in the Third World will die before the age of five. In one year there will be 7.6 million deaths from impure water. Another 3.5 million will die from communicable diseases. One-third of these are from diseases like whooping cough, diphtheria, tuberculosis and other diseases that are almost extinct in the United States and Canada.

The figure of 10.6 million deaths is so large that it is almost beyond comprehension. An illustration helps put it in context. We were all shocked a few years ago when a Korean 747 jet was shot down and all the crew and passengers killed; and in a subsequent disaster, when a Pan Am flight was blown out of the air over Lockerbie, Scotland. These were dreadful tragedies that attracted widespread and prolonged attention. Yet the number of children dying needlessly each year from impure water and lack of immunization is the equivalent of one Boeing 747 carrying 360 passengers being shot down every 18 minutes, day and night, 365 days a year. If these hypothetical planes were filled with American kids or Canadian, English, French or German, someone would move heaven and earth to do something about it. Some progress is being made but it's at a snail's pace. The world's indifference is called the silent tragedy.

If this all sounds a little preachy I suppose that is fair comment but less so in the context of its wider meaning. I am not one who draws a clear distinction between moral law and enlightened self-interest. When Moses delivered the Ten Commandments he may have hoped that they would put the fear of the Lord into the hearts of the Children of Israel. But another interpretation of the decalogue might be that it reflects the wisdom of a loving parent who says: "My children, to the extent that you are able to live according to these precepts you will save yourselves a lot of grief."

I believe that the way we have operated our economies for the last couple of decades, and the way we continue to operate them, fails just about any test of morality or common sense that could be applied. The flip-side of the coin is that we have caused ourselves a lot of unnecessary grief in lives ruined, families broken up, dreams shattered and opportunities lost. We have been sowing the wind and reaping the whirlwind.

The whirlwind we are reaping is a kind of casino mentality, both literally and figuratively. Periodic recessions reduce the revenues of states and provinces so they look to lotteries and casinos for extra revenue. First Nations' bands are faced with inadequate job opportunities for their members so they turn to casinos for jobs and revenue. The banks find the pickings from their traditional business a little thin so they start writing derivatives which create new and uncertain risks. As Henry Kaufman said in a talk delivered before the City of London Conference on Derivatives, in October 1993, "If, as many in senior management maintain, the bulk of the profits comes from 'running the casino' rather than 'playing at the tables', that should be backed up with hard numbers. Otherwise, the suspicion is that profits stem mainly from position-taking, which entails market exposure, and not from merely marrying bids and offers."[11]

This kind of activity has one thing in common – for every winner there is a loser. Contrast this with activity that creates real wealth which is a win-win situation for investor, worker and tax-collectors alike. Surely the object of a just, caring society should be to allow everyone to accumulate a little stake rather than to "clean their clock". Most people don't ask for the mansions and conspicuous consumption of the rich. The majority, especially the poor, would settle for the five basics which include adequate food, clothing, shelter, telephone and television. Millions in the Third World would settle for much less.

So the options are clear. We can continue on the present course until the financial super-structure crashes all around us with earth-shattering consequences for millions, or we can reform the system in a way that will provide stability and opportunity. Even then, however, the kind of society that most of us dream of will not come automatically. The mess we're in is a result of the attitudes and actions of men and women. We are responsible for the failure of the system to meet the needs and aspirations of the unhappy minority. Even a reformed system will not achieve its potential unless good men and women make it work well. The policies recommended in this book are a good place to start. The future of the U.S. economy, and of its influence on the world economy, is more important than the future profitability of the banks which will, no doubt, cope quite nicely by one means or another. But neither the U.S. economy nor, by extension, the world economy can achieve its potential without a revolutionary change of heart and mind on the part of the people who manage it. We have to translate the lip-service we pay to honesty, justice and compassion into the reality of the marketplace. Some would call it the moral thing to do; others would just say it is the essence of common sense.

NOTES

Chapter 1: A Tragic Divorce

1.   Soule, George, *Ideas of the Great Economists*, A Mentor Book published by arrangement with The Viking Press, Inc. 1952, p. 65.
2.   *Ibid.*
3.   Holy Bible, The New King James Version, Thomas Nelson Inc., 1983, Acts 2, Verses 44-45, p. 1107.
4.   Hepburn, Bob, "Israel's kibbutz movement in crisis", in *The Toronto Star*, Sunday, January 30, 1994, p. E5.
5.   Arundel Lodge, Lake Muskoka, Ontario, Canada.
6.   DeMara, Bruce and Bragg, Rebecca, "Help East Bloc now Irish president urges, *The Toronto Star*, Tuesday, August 23, 1994, p. A16.

Chapter 2: Money, Funny Money and Phony Money

1.   Holy Bible, The New King James Version, Thomas Nelson Inc., 1983, Genesis 47, Verses 13-17, p. 48.
2.   Lui, Francis T., "Cagan's Hypothesis and the First Nationwide Inflation of Paper Money in World History", Journal of Political Economy, Vol. 91, #6, 1983, pp. 1067-74, in *Major Inflations in History*, Forrest H. Capie (ed.), Aldershot: Edward Elgar Publishing Limited, 1991, pp. 210-212.
3.   *Ibid.*
4.   Chaffers, William, *Gilda Aurifabrorum: A History of English Goldsmiths and Plateworkers, and Their Marks Stamped on Plate*, London: Reeves & Turner, [1800], p. 210.
5.   *Ibid.*
6.   Hixson, William F., *Triumph of the Bankers: Money and Banking in the Eighteenth and Nineteenth Centuries*, Westport: Praeger Publishers, 1993, p. 46.

7. *Ibid*, p. 60.
8. Nettles, Curtis P., *The Money Supply of the American Colonies before 1720*, New York: Augustus M. Kelley, 1964, p. 169.
9. Powell, Ellis T., *The Evolution of the Money Market - 1385-1915*, New York: Augustus M. Kelley, 1966, p. 197.
10. *Ibid.*, pp. 117-118.
11. *Ibid.*, p. 129.
12. Innis, Mary Quayle, *An Economic History of Canada*, Toronto: The Ryerson Press, 1935, p. 28.
13. Lester, Richard A., "Currency Issues to Overcome Depressions in Pennsylvania, 1723 and 1729", *The Journal of Political Economy*, Vol. 46, June 1938, p. 326.
14. Hixson, William F., *Triumph of the Bankers*, op. cit., p. 46.
15. Lester, Richard A., "Currency Issues to Overcome Depressions in Pennsylvania, 1723 and 1729", op. cit., p. 338.
16. *Ibid.*, p. 341.
17. Smith, Adam, *Wealth of Nations*, New York: P.F. Collier and Son, 1909, p. 266.
18. Nettles, Curtis P., *The Money Supply of the American Colonies before 1720*, op. cit., p. 265.
19. Ferguson, E. James, *The Power of the Purse: A History of American Public Finance, 1776-1790*, Chapel Hill: University of North Carolina Press, 1961, p. 16.
20. Hixson, William F., *Triumph of the Bankers*, op. cit., p. 81.
21. Franklin, Benjamin, *The Writings of Benjamin Franklin*, Albert Henry Smyth (ed.), New York: Macmillan, 1907, (9), pp. 231-233.
22. Mitchell, Broadus, *The Price of Independence*, New York: Oxford University Press, 1974, pp. 401-403.
23. Hixson, William F., *Triumph of the Bankers*, op. cit., p. 80.
24. *Ibid*.

25.   Morris, Richard B., *The Forging of the Union 1781-1789*, New York: Harper & Row, 1987, p. 155.

26.   Hixson, William F., *Triumph of the Bankers*, op. cit., p. 115.

27.   Sumner, William Graham, *A History of American Currency*, New York: Augustus M. Kelley, 1968, p. 123.

28.   Gouge, William M., *A Short History of Paper Money and Banking in the United States*, New York: Augustus M. Kelley, Part II, 1968, p. 45.

29.   Angell, Norman, *The Story of Money*, New York: Frederick A. Stokes Co., 1929, p. 294.

30.   Hixson, William, F., *Triumph of the Bankers*, op. cit., p. 150.

31.   Bordo, Michael D., "Gold Standard", in *Encyclopedia of Economics*, David R. Henderson (ed.), New York: Warner Books, Inc., 1993, p. 359.

32.   *Ibid.*

33.   For budget discussion see U.K. Parliamentary Debates, Vol. clxxxiii, col. 55.

34.   *Ibid.*

35.   Bordo, Michael D., "Gold Standard", op. cit., p. 360.

36.   Galbraith, John Kenneth, *Money, Whence it Came, Where it Went*, Boston: Houghton Mifflin Company, 1975, p. 10-11.

Chapter 3: Phony Money Reigns Supreme

1.   Stiglitz, Joseph E., "Information" in *Encyclopedia of Economics*, David R. Henderson (ed.), New York: Warner Books, Inc., 1993, p. 18.

2.   Schwartz, Anna J., "Money Supply" in *Encyclopedia of Economics*, David R. Henderson (ed.), New York: Warner Books, Inc., 1993, p. 365.

3.   *Seventy-Ninth Annual Report of the Board of Governors of the Federal Reserve System*, 1992, p. 281.

4.   Source: International Financial Statistics Yearbook, IMF June 1993.

5.   Saul, John Ralston, *Voltaire's Bastards*, pp. 376-377. Copyright © John Ralston Saul, 1992. Reprinted by permission of Penguin Books Canada Limited.

6.   Grant, James, *Money of the Mind: Borrowing and Lending in America from the Civil War to Michael Milken*, New York: Farrar Straus Giroux, 1992, p. 414.

7.   Associated Press, "Japanese banks lend Viacom $2-billion", in *The Globe and Mail*, Friday, June 17, 1994, p. B7.

8.   Yakabuski, Konrad, "Banks win big in Rogers bid", in *The Toronto Star*, Tuesday, February 15, 1994, p. D11.

9.   Quill, Greg, "Rogers hike will make rate country's highest", in *The Toronto Star*, Wednesday, July 13, 1994, p. D6.

10. *The State of the World's Children, 1992, Summary*, New York: Oxford University Press, pp. 8-11.

11. *Ibid.*

12. Smith, Randall; Herman, Tom; and Gottschalk, Earl C. Jr., in "Bond Market's Rout, The Worst Since 1987, Stuns Many Investors - Even Big, Savvy Players Get A Pounding as Leverage Proves to Be Dangerous - But Many Hold On and Wait", in *The Wall Street Journal*, Thursday, April 7, 1994, p. A1.

13. Jereski, Laura, "High Leverage at Kidder Could Lead to Headaches", in *The Wall Street Journal*, Monday, June 6, 1994, p. C1.

14. Lipin, Steven; Granito, Barbara Donnelly; and Scism, Leslie, in "Bankers Trust Thrives Pitching Derivatives, But Climate Is Shifting - Losses by Clients Like P&G May Crimp Plan to Move To Relationship Banking - Some Intense Pressure to Sell", in *The Wall Street Journal*, Friday, April 22, 1994, p. A1

15. *Ibid.*, p. A4.

16. "You'd better ask Murphy", in *The Banker*, February 1993, p. 48.

17. Partridge, John, "Ottawa to leave derivatives trade free of red tape", in *The Globe and Mail*, Tuesday, May 10, 1994, p. B1.
18. Samuelson, Robert J., "Great Depression" in *Encyclopedia of Economics*, David R. Henderson (ed.), New York: Warner Books, Inc., 1993, p. 202.

Chapter 4: An Infinitely Silly System

1. Hixson, William F., *Triumph of the Bankers: Money and Banking in the Eighteenth and Nineteenth Centuries*, Westport: Praeger Publishers, 1993, p. 81.
2. *Ibid.*, pp. 45-58.
3. Friedman, Milton and Schwartz, Anna Jacobson, *A Monetary History of the United States 1867-1960*, Princeton: Princeton University Press, 1963, p. 322.
4. Day, Donald, *Will Rogers: A Biography*, New York: David McKay Company, Inc., 1962, p. 285.
5. Friedman, Milton and Schwartz, Anna Jacobson, *A Monetary History of the United States 1867-1960*, op. cit.
6. *Ibid.*, pp. 327-328.
7. *Maclean's Magazine*, July 1, 1933 as reprinted in *The Journal of Economic History*, Goldin, Claudia, and Hohenberg, Paul (eds.), The Economic History Association, University of Pennsylvania, June 1987, Vol. XLVII, No. 2, p. 415.
8. Source: Flow of Fund Accounts Financial Assets and Liabilities Year End – Tables L2 through L4, Federal Reserve System, Washington, D.C.
9. Meltzer, Allan H., "Monetarism", in *Encyclopedia of Economics*, Henderson, David R. (ed.), New York: Warner Books, Inc., 1993, p. 128.
10. *Annual Report of the Council of Economic Advisers*, February 1983, p. 21.
11. Sawhill, Isabel V., "Poverty in the United States", in *Encyclopedia of Economics*, David R. Henderson (ed.), New York: Warner Books, Inc., 1993, p. 58.

12.   Hixson, William F., *A Matter of Interest: Reexamining Money, Debt, and Real Economic Growth*, New York: Praeger Publishers, 1991, pp. 173-174.

13.   Cooper, Richard N., "A Monetary System for the Future", in *Foreign Affairs*, Vol. 63, #1, Fall 1984, pp. 166-184.

Chapter 5: Nothing New Under the Sun

1.   Friedman, Milton, "A Monetary and Fiscal Framework for Economic Stability", in *American Economic Review*, XXXVIII, June 1948.

2.   Friedman, Milton, *A Program for Monetary Stability*, New York: Fordham University Press, 1959, p. 65.

3.   *Ibid.*   Henry C. Simons, "A Positive Program for Laissez Faire: Some Proposals for a Liberal Economic Policy," in his *Economic Policy for A Free Society* (Chicago, 1948), pp. 62-5 (first published as "Public Policy Pamphlet, No. 15, ed. Harry D. Gideonse (Chicago, 1934); Lloyd W. Mints, *Monetary Policy for a Competitive Society* (New York, 1950), pp. 186-87. Albert G. Hart, "The 'Chicago Plan' of Banking Reform," *Review of Economic Studies*, 2 (1935), pp. 104-16. Reprinted in Friedrich A. Lutz and Lloyd W. Mints (eds.), *Readings in Monetary Theory* (New York, 1951), pp. 437-56.

4.   Fisher, Irving, *100% Money*, New York: The Adelphi Company, 1935.

5.   Hixson, William F., *Triumph of the Bankers: Money and Banking in the Eighteenth and Nineteenth Centuries*, Westport: Praeger Publishers, 1993, p. 49.

6.   Nicolay, John G., and Hay, John (eds.) *Abraham Lincoln: Complete Works*, New York: The Century Co., 1907, 2: p. 264.

7.   Hixson, William F., *Triumph of the Bankers*, op. cit., p. 134.

8.   Hammond, Bray, *Sovereignty and an Empty Purse*, Princeton: Princeton University Press, 1970, p. 192.

9.   Campbell, Alexander, *The True Greenback*, Chicago: Republican Books, 1868, p. 31.

10.   McCulloch, Hugh, *Men and Measures of Half a Century*, New York: Charles Scribner's Sons, 1888, p. 201.

11.   Myers, Margaret G., *A Financial History of the United States*, New York: Columbia University Press, 1970, p. 198.

12.   McPherson, Edward (ed.), *A Hand-Book of Politics*, New York: Da Capo Publishing Corp., 1972, p. 271.

13.   Low, Solon E., *Hansard*, Vol. 2, 5th Session, March 10, 1949, p. 1334.

14.   Blackmore, John H., *Hansard*, Vol. 6, 3rd Session, July 24, 1956, p. 6368.

15.   Confirmed in telephone conversation with Robert Thompson on July 7, 1994.

16.   McIvor, R. Craig, *Canadian Monetary, Banking and Fiscal Development*, Toronto: The Macmillan Company of Canada Limited, 1958, p. 160.

17.   Simons, Henry C., *Economic Policy for a Free Society*, Chicago: University of Chicago Press, 1948, pp. 65-66.

18.   Grant, Jordan B., *Reintegrating Monetary Policy Into the Economic Tool Kit*, January 24, 1994.

19.   Information provided by Professor John H. Hotson, Executive Director, The Committee on Monetary and Economic Reform, August 8, 1994.

20.   Biddell, Jack L., *A Self-Reliant Future for Canada*, Thornhill: LNC Publications, 1993, p. 98.

21.   DeGeer, Gerald Gratton, Mayor of Vancouver, Dec. 1934 for 2 years; Dec. 1946 for 2 years but passed away Aug. 1947.

22.   Cowles, Virginia, *The Rothschilds: A Family of Fortune*, New York: Alfred A. Knopf, Inc., 1973.

23.   *"Michael" Journal*, Quebec: July-August, 1994, p. 17.

24.   Fisher, Irving, *100% Money*, New York: The Adelphi Company, 1935, p. 20.

25.   Friedman, Milton, *A Program For Monetary Stability*, op. cit., pp. 65-66.

26.   *Ibid.*, p. 75.

Chapter 6: Make Love Not War

1.   Friedman, Milton, "A Second Industrial Revolution", speech given at the 9th Dr. Harold Walter Siebens Lecture, The Fraser Institute, Vancouver, B.C., May 18, 1994.
2.   The OECD Jobs Study, "Facts-Analysis-Strategies, Unemployment in the OECD Area 1950-1995", Organisation for Economic Co-operation and Development, 1994, p. 10.
3.   *Our Common Future, Report of the World Commission on Environment and Development*, Oxford: Oxford University Press, 1987.
4.   Trefil, James, "Earth's Future Climate" in *Our World, Our Environment*, 1991, p. 9, reprinted from *Smithsonian* Magazine, 1990.
5.   *Ibid*, p. 15.
6.   Stilkind, Jerry, USIA Staff Writer "EPA Says U.S. Air Quality Improved again in 1992", November 3, 1993.
7.   *Ibid.*
8.   Worsnop, Richard L., "Water Quality" in *CQ Researcher*, February 11, 1994.
9.   Browner, Carol M., Administrator United States Environmental Protection Agency, press release on "Proposed Water Quality Guidance for the Great Lakes", March 31, 1993.
10.   Statistics Canada 1991, 360 kg. of solid waste per person.
11.   "After the Trash Can", in *The Garbage Primer*, Lyons & Burford, Publishers, 1993, p. 4.
12.   *Ibid*, p. 7.
13.   Pearce, Kevin, "The U.S. Disposes of the Way It Disposes - By Recycling" in *Environment The Next Frontier*, a U.S. Information Agency Publication, p. 19.
14.   *Ibid*, p. 18.

15. Smolowe, Jill, "Giving the cold shoulder", in *Time*, December 6, 1993, p. 28.

16. Leo, John, "Distorting the homeless debate", in *U.S. News & World Report*, November 8, 1993, p. 27.

17. Smolowe, Jill, "Giving the cold shoulder", op. cit.

18. *Ibid.*

19. Thomas, Paulette, "Fed Lifts Short-Term Rates By Half a Percentage Point", in *The Wall Street Journal*, Wednesday, August 17, 1994, p. A2.

20. "Literacy Levels Deficient for 90 Million U.S. Adults", in *United States Department of Education News*, September 8, 1993.

21. Eck, Alan, "Job-related education and training: their impact on earnings", in *Monthly Labor Review*, October 1993, p. 37.

22. Hellyer, Paul, *Damn the Torpedoes*, Toronto: McClelland & Stewart Inc., 1990, pp. 134-136.

23. Reich, Robert B., *The Work of Nations: Preparing Ourselves for 21st Century Capitalism*, New York: Alfred A. Knopf, Inc., 1991, p. 254.

24. Hellyer, Paul, *Report of The Task Force on Housing and Urban Development*, Ottawa: The Queen's Printer, January, 1969, p. 11.

25. "Hell is a dying city", Editorial in the *Economist*, November 6, 1993, p. 13.

26. *Ibid.*

27. Sowell, Thomas, "The unheavenly city", in *American Spectator*, February, 1994, p. 45.

28. Cohen, Warren, "Cities try to bring home the bacon; job creation is still a struggle for urban America", in *U.S. News & World Report*, January 31, 1994, p. 59.

29. Sowell, Thomas, "The unheavenly city", op. cit.

30. The OECD Jobs Study, op. cit., p. 29.

Chapter 7: A 50% Solution

1.   Chaffers, William, *Gilda Aurifabrorum: A History of English Goldsmiths and Plateworkers, and Their Marks Stamped on Plate*, London: Reeves & Turner, [1800], pp. 210-211.
2.   *Ibid.*
3.   Fisher, Irving, *100% Money*, New York: The Adelphi Company, 1935, p. 8.
4.   *Ibid.*, pp. 10-12.
5.   Friedman, Milton, in a footnote reply to a letter from William F. Hixson, November 9, 1983.
6.   Friedman, Milton, in a letter to Professor John H. Hotson, February 3, 1986.
7.   *Ibid.*
8.   Sources: Laurence H. Meyer & Associates, Limited, and Informetrica Limited.
9.   *Ibid.*
10.   Pope, William Henry, "The Value of the Dollar".
11.   Sources: Laurence H. Meyer & Associates, Limited, Informetrica Limited and Statistics Canada.
12.   *Ibid.*

Chapter 8: A False and Inadequate Diagnosis

1.   Kenneth Boulding, 1969, as quoted by Arthur B. Laffer, "Trade Credit and the Money Market", in *Journal of Political Economy*, Vol. 78, No. 2, March/April 1970, p. 239.
2.   As quoted by Alan S. Blinder, "Keynesian Economics" in *Encyclopedia of Economics*, David R. Henderson (ed.), New York: Warner Books, Inc., 1993, p. 118.
3.   Friedman, Milton, *Monetarist Economics*, Oxford: Basil Blackwell Ltd., 1991, pp. 14-18.
4.   *Ibid.*, p. 16.
5.   *Ibid.*, p 13.
6.   Bladen, Vincent, "Prescribing Remedies for Inflation", in *The Globe and Mail*, August 29, 1973.

7.   Lekachman, Robert, *Inflation: The Permanent Problem of Boom and Bust*, New York: Vintage Books, 1973, p. 37.

8.   *Annual Report of the Council of Economic Advisers*, Washington, D.C., January 1981, p. 39.

9.   Samuelson, Paul A., *Economics*, 9th ed., New York: McGraw-Hill Book Co., 1973, p. 829.

10.   *Bank of Canada Annual Report*, February 27, 1981, p. 16.

11.   O.E.C.D. Main Economic Indicators, 1965-70.

12.   *Economic Report of the President*, January 1981, pp. 7-8.

13.   *Ibid.*, p. 8.

14.   *Ibid.*

15.   Friedman, Milton, *A Program for Monetary Stability*, New York: Fordham University Press, 1959.

16.   The letter was written by John Crispo and Douglas Hartle of the University of Toronto and signed by all seventeen.

17.   Harriss, C. Lowell, "Causes and Effects of Inflation", in *Inflation: Long-Term Problems*, New York: The Academy of Political Science, 1975, p. 11.

18.   *Ibid.*, pp. 11-12.

19.   *Annual Report of the Council of Economic Advisers*, February 1982, pp. 95-96.

20.   *Ibid.*, p. 95.

21.   Crozier, Robert B. , *Deficit Financing and Inflation: Facts and Fictions*, The Conference Board in Canada, March 1976.

22.   *Economic Report of the President*, January 1981, pp. 41-42.

23.   *Annual Report of the Council of Economic Advisers*, February 1982, p. 99.

24.   Harriss, C. Lowell, "Causes and Effects of Inflation", *op. cit.*, pp. 11-12.

25.   *Congressional Quarterly*, 1975, p. 14.

26.   *Ibid.*

27.   *Ibid.*

28.   *Economic Report of the President*, January 1980, p. 3.
29.   *Annual Report of the Council of Economic Advisers*, February 1983, p. 225.
30.   Mundell, Robert A., Professor of Economics at Cambridge, and Arthur B. Laffer, then of the University of Chicago Graduate School of Business.
31.   *Bank of Canada Annual Report*, Ottawa, March 1981, p. 11.

Chapter 9: The Schizo Economy

1.   1982 Census of Manufacturers, *Concentration Ratios in Manufacturing*, Washington D.C.: U.S. Department of Commerce, 1985.
2.   Stigler, George J., "Monopoly & Oligopoly by Merger", *American Economic Review Supplement*, XL, 1950, pp. 23 ff.
3.   Low, Richard E. (ed.), *The Economics of Antitrust: Competition and Monopoly,* Englewood Cliffs: Prentice-Hall Inc., 1968, p. 6.
4.   Caves, Richard E., *American Industry: Structure, Conduct, Performance*, 2nd ed. Englewood Cliffs, N.J.: Prentice-Hall Inc., 1968, p. 6.
5.   Munkirs, John R., *The Transformation of American Capitalism From Competitive Market Structures to Centralized Sector Planning*, New York: M.E. Sharpe, Inc., 1985.
6.   Reynolds, Morgan O., "Labor Unions" in *Encyclopedia of Economics*, David R. Henderson (ed.), New York: Warner Books, Inc., 1993, p. 494.
7.   *Ibid.*
8.   Jones, Aubrey, *The New Inflation: The Politics of Prices and Incomes*, London: Andre Deutsch, 1973.
9.   McCarthy, W.E.J.; O'Brien, J.F., and V.G. Dowd, *Wage Inflation and Wage Leadership: A Study of the Role of Key Wage Bargains in the Irish System of Collective Bargaining,* Dublin: Cahill & Co. Ltd., 1975, p. 11

10.   *Annual Report of the Council of Economic Advisers*, Washington, D.C., January 1981, p. 34.
11.   Source: Q.&W. - OECD National Accounts; P=CPI in IMF Financial Statistics Yearbook. Labour Force - OECD Labour Force Statistics.
12.   Friedman, Milton, and Friedman, Rose D., *Free to Choose: A Personal Statement*, New York: Avon Books, 1981, p. 11.
13.   Weintraub, Sidney, *Capitalism's Inflation and Unemployment Crisis: Beyond Monetarism and Keynesiasm*, New York: Addison-Wesley Publishing Company, Inc., 1978, p. 104.
14.   Friedman, Milton, and Friedman, Rose D., *Free to Choose: A Personal Statement*, op. cit., p. 251.
15.   *Business Week*, March 31, 1980, p. 80.

Chapter 10:   An Incomes Policy for Monopolies and Oligopolies

1.   *Economic Report of the President*, January 1979, p. 4.
2.   *Annual Report of the Council of Economic Advisers*, Washington, D.C., January 1979, p. 82.
3.   Decision by U.S. District Judge Barrington Parker, May 31, 1979.
4.   *Annual Report of the Council of Economic Advisers*, January 1980, pp. 36-38.
5.   *Ibid.*
6.   Mill, John Stuart, edited with an introduction by Sir William J. Ashley, *Principles of Political Economy with some of their Applications to Social Philosophy*, New York: Augustus M. Kelley, 1909, p. 963.
7.   The prediction was stated in a press release issued by Action Canada.
8.   Galbraith, John Kenneth, *The New Industrial State*, Boston: Houghton Mifflin Co., 1971.
9.   On a $15,000 house.

10.   Wage drift is an arbitrary system of job reclassification that could nullify the intent of wage guidelines or controls.
11.   "Time for an Incomes Policy", Lead Editorial in *The New York Times*, Thursday, May 5, 1983.
12.   *Annual Report of the Council of Economic Advisers*, January 1981, pp. 61-65.
13.   *Ibid.*
14.   *Ibid.*
15.   *Ibid.*
16.   Source: Informetrica Limited.

Chapter 11: Other Things

1.   Courtesy of Professor Wallace Peterson, George Holmes Professor of Economics Emeritus, University of Nebraska - Lincoln.
2.   Haliechuk, Rick, "Deposit safety must come first: bank group chief", in *The Toronto Star*, Tuesday, March 29, 1994, p. B3
3.   *The Toronto Stock Exchange Fact Sheet*, "Findings of the TSE-ESOP Database", 1989.
4.   Special to *New Federalist*, "Global Panic Spreads - And It Is Over the Economy, Stupid", April 6, 1994.
5.   *Ibid.*
6.   Gorman, Linda, "Minimum Wages" in *Encyclopedia of Economics*, David R. Henderson (ed.), New York: Warner Books, Inc., 1993, p. 499.
7.   *Ibid.*

Chapter 12: A Star to Steer By

1.   Friedman, Milton and Schwartz, Anna Jacobson, *A Monetary History of the United States 1867-1960*, Princeton: Princeton University Press, 1963.
2.   The Smoot-Hawley Bill was enacted by Congress in 1930.

3.   "The Church Faces the Challenge", The Report of the Church of Scotland Commission on Communism, London: Longmans, Green and Co. Ltd., 1955, p. 9.

4.   Holy Bible, The New King James Version, Thomas Nelson Inc., 1983, I John, 4, Verse 20.

5.   Keller, Robert J., O.P., PhD, Director of the Catholic (Newman) Center at Emory University, Atlanta, Georgia, in a letter to the author dated April 29, 1944.

6.   *Ibid.*

7.   Steinbach, Alexander Alan, *What is Judaism*, New York: Behrman Jewish Book House, 1937, p. 40.

8.   Smith, Jane I., Vice President and Dean of Academic Affairs, Iliff School of Theology, Denver, Colorado, in a letter to the author dated April 20, 1994.

9.   "Buddhist Ethics", in *The New Encyclopaedia Britannica*, Encyclopaedia Britannica, Inc., 15th Edition, Volume 3, , 1981, p. 429.

10.   Beck, Peggy V. and Walters, Anna L., *The Sacred Ways of Knowledge Sources of Life*, Navajo Community College Press, 1977, p. 25.

11.   Kaufman, Henry, "Financial Derivatives and their Risks", a talk delivered before City of London Conference on Derivatives, London, England, October 14, 1993.

Appendix A

Reserve Requirements of Depository Institutions[1]

Type of deposit[2]	Requirements	
	Percent of deposits	Effective date
Net transaction accounts[3]		
$0 million–$46.8 million	3	12/15/92
More than $46.8 million	10	12/15/92
Nonpersonal time deposits[4]	0	12/27/90
Eurocurrency liabilities[5]	0	12/27/90

1. Reserve requirements in effect on December 31, 1992. Required reserves must be held in the form of deposits with Federal Reserve Banks or vault cash. Nonmember institutions may maintain reserve balances with a Federal Reserve Bank indirectly on a pass-through basis with certain approved institutions. For previous reserve requirements, see earlier editions of the *Annual Report* or the *Federal Reserve Bulletin*. Under provisions of the Monetary Control Act, depository institutions include commercial banks, mutual savings banks, savings and loan associations, credit unions, agencies and branches of foreign banks, and Edge corporations.

2. The Garn–St Germain Depository Institutions Act of 1982 (Public Law 97–320) requires that $2 million of reservable liabilities of each depository institution be subject to a zero percent reserve requirement. The Board is to adjust the amount of reservable liabilities subject to this zero percent reserve requirement each year for the succeeding calendar year by 80 percent of the percentage increase in the total reservable liabilities of all depository institutions measured on an annual basis as of June 30. No corresponding adjustment is to be made in the event of a decrease. On December 15, 1992, the exemption was raised from $3.6 million to $3.8 million. The exemption applies in the following order: (1) net negotiable order of withdrawal (NOW) accounts (NOW accounts less allowable deductions); and (2) net other transaction accounts. The exemption applies only to accounts that would be subject to a 3 percent reserve requirement.

3. Transaction accounts include all deposits against which the account holder is permitted to make withdrawals by negotiable or transferable instruments, payment orders of withdrawal, and telephone and preauthorized transfers in excess of three per month for the purpose of making payments to third persons or others. However, money market deposit accounts (MMDAs) and similar accounts subject to the rules that permit no more than six preauthorized, automatic, or other transfers per month, of which no more than three can be checks, are not transaction accounts (such accounts are savings deposits).

The Monetary Control Act of 1980 requires that the amount of transaction accounts against which the 3 percent reserve requirement applies be modified annually by 80 percent of the percentage change in transaction accounts held by all depository institutions, determined as of June 30 each year. Effective December 15, 1992 for institutions reporting quarterly and December 22, 1992 for institutions reporting weekly, the amount was increased from $42.2 million to $46.8 million.

4. For institutions that report weekly, the reserve requirement on nonpersonal time deposits with an original maturity of less than 1½ years was reduced from 3 percent to 1½ percent for the maintenance period that began December 13, 1990, and to zero for the maintenance period that began December 27, 1990. The reserve requirement on nonpersonal time deposits with an original maturity of 1½ years or more has been zero since October 6, 1983.

For institutions that report quarterly, the reserve requirement on nonpersonal time deposits with an original maturity of less than 1½ years was reduced from 3 percent to zero on January 17, 1991.

5. The reserve requirement on Euroccurency liabilities was reduced from 3 percent to zero in the same manner and on the same dates as were the reserve requirement on nonpersonal time deposits with an original maturity of less than 1½ years (see note 4).

BIBLIOGRAPHY

Angell, Norman, *The Story of Money*, New York: Frederick A. Stokes Co., 1929.

Beck, Peggy V. and Walters, Anna L., *The Sacred Ways of Knowledge Sources of Life*, Navajo Community College Press, 1977.

Biddell, Jack L., *A Self-Reliant Future For Canada*, Thornhill: LNC Publications, 1993.

Campbell, Alexander, *The True Greenback*, Chicago: Republican Books, 1868.

Caves, Richard E., *American Industry: Structure, Conduct, Performance*, 2nd ed. Englewood Cliffs: Prentice-Hall Inc., 1968.

Chaffers, William, *Gilda Aurifabrorum: A History of English Goldsmiths and Plateworkers, and Their Marks Stamped on Plate*, London: Reeves & Turner, [1800].

Cowles, Virginia, *The Rothschilds: A Family of Fortune*, New York: Alfred A. Knopf, Inc., 1973.

Day, Donald, *Will Rogers: A Biography*, New York: David McKay Company, Inc., 1962.

Ferguson, E. James, *The Power of the Purse: A History of American Public Finance, 1776-1790*, Chapel Hill: University of North Carolina Press, 1961.

Fisher, Irving, *100% Money*, New York: The Adelphi Company, 1935.

Franklin, Benjamin, *The Writings of Benjamin Franklin*, Albert Henry Smyth (ed.), New York: Macmillan, 1907.

Friedman, Milton, *Monetarist Economics*, Oxford: Basil Blackwell Ltd., 1991.

Friedman, Milton, *A Program For Monetary Stability*, New York: Fordham University Press, 1959.

Friedman, Milton and Rose D. Friedman, *Free to Choose: A Personal Statement*, New York: Avon Books, 1981.

Friedman, Milton and Schwartz, Anna Jacobson, *A Monetary History of the United States 1967-1960*, Princeton: Princeton University Press, 1963.

Galbraith, John Kenneth, *Money, Whence it Came, Where it Went*, Boston: Houghton Mifflin Company, 1975.

Galbraith, John Kenneth, *The New Industrial State*, Boston: Houghton Mifflin Co., 1971.

Gouge, William M., *A Short History of Paper Money and Banking in the United States*, New York: Augustus M. Kelley, Part II, 1968.

Grant, James, *Money of the Mind: Borrowing and Lending in America from the Civil War to Michael Milken*, New York: Farrar Straus Giroux, 1992.

Hammond, Bray, *Sovereignty and an Empty Purse*, Princeton: Princeton University Press, 1970.

Hellyer, Paul, *Damn the Torpedoes*, Toronto: McClelland & Stewart Inc., 1990.

Henderson, David R. (ed), *Encyclopedia of Economics*, New York: Warner Books, Inc., 1993.

Hixson, William F., *Triumph of the Bankers: Money and Banking in the Eighteenth and Nineteenth Centuries*, Westport: Praeger Publishers, 1993.

Hixson, William F., *A Matter of Interest: Reexamining Money, Debt, and Real Economic Growth*, New York: Praeger Publishers, 1991.

Innis, Mary Quayle, *An Economic History of Canada*, Toronto: The Ryerson Press, 1935.

Jones, Aubrey, *The New Inflation: The Politics of Prices and Incomes*, London: Andre Deutsch, 1973.

Lekachman, Robert, *Inflation: The Permanent Problem of Boom and Bust*, New York: Vintage Books, 1973.

Low, Richard E. (ed.), *The Economics of Antitrust, Competition and Monopoly*, Englewood Cliffs: Prentice-Hall Inc., 1968.

McCarthy, W.E.J.; O'Brien, J.F., and V.G. Dowd, *Wage Inflation and Wage Leadership: A Study of the Role of Key Wage Bargains in the Irish System of Collective Bargaining*, Dublin: Cahill & Co. Ltd., 1975.

McCulloch, Hugh, *Men and Measures of Half a Century*, New York: Charles Scribner's Sons, 1888.

McIvor, R. Craig, *Canadian Monetary Banking and Fiscal Development*, Toronto: The Macmillan Company of Canada Limited, 1958.

McPherson, Edward (ed.), *A Hand-Book of Politics*, New York: Da Capo Publishing Co., 1972, p. 271.

Mill, John Stuart, edited with an introduction by Sir William J. Ashley, *Principles of Political Economy with some of their Applications to Social Philosophy*, New York: Augustus M. Kelley, 1909.

Mitchell, Broadus, *The Price of Independence*, New York: Oxford University Press, 1974.

Morris, Richard B., *The Forging of the Union 1781-1789*, New York: Harper & Row, 1987.

Munkirs, John R., *The Transformation of American Capitalism From Competitive Market Structures to Centralized Sector Planning*, New York: M.E. Sharpe, Inc., 1985.

Myers, Margaret G., *A Financial History of the United States*, New York: Columbia University Press, 1970.

Nettles, Curtis P., *The Money Supply of the American Colonies before 1720*, New York: Augustus M. Kelley, 1964.

Nicolay, John G., and Hay, John, (eds). *Abraham Lincoln: Complete Works*, New York: The Century Co., 1907.

Powell, Ellis T., *The Evolution of the Money Market - 1385-1915*, New York: Augustus M. Kelley, 1966.

Reich, Robert B., *The Work of Nations: Preparing Ourselves for 21st Century Capitalism*, New York: Alfred A. Knopf, Inc., 1991.

Samuelson, Paul A., *Economics*, 9th ed., New York: McGraw-Hill Book Co., 1973.

Saul, John Ralston, *Voltaire's Bastards: The Dictatorship of Reason in the West*, Toronto: Penguin Books, 1993.

Simons, Henry, C., *Economic Policy for a Free Society*, Chicago: University of Chicago Press, 1948.

Smith, Adam, *Wealth of Nations*, New York: P.F. Collier and Son, 1909.

Soule, George, *Ideas of the Great Economists*, A Mentor Book published by arrangement with The Viking Press, Inc., 1952.

Steinbach, Alexander Alan, *What is Judaism*, New York: Behrman Jewish Book House, 1937.

Sumner, William Graham, *A History of American Currency*, New York: Augustus M. Kelley, 1968.

Weintraub, Sidney, *Capitalism's Inflation and Unemployment Crisis: Beyond Monetarism and Keynesiasm*, New York: Addison-Wesley Publishing Company, Inc., 1978.

INDEX